PRAISE FOR *THE SACRED JOURNEY*

"Life is a journey" is a widely recognized expression. Yet the metaphor is meaningless unless we experience the physical, bodily movement of travel. In *The Sacred Journey*, Charles Foster ably links the metaphorical to the physical, and thus relinks body and spirit, soles and souls.

S. Brent Plate
Cofounder and Managing Editor
Material Religion: The Journal of Objects, Art, and Belief

A lively, original, and idiosyncratic approach to the subject of pilgrimage that captures the motif of journey at the heart of the Christian faith, and which should have all of its readers reaching for their boots and backpacks.

Rev. Dr. Ian Bradley
Reader in Church History and Practical Theology,
University of St. Andrews
Author, *Pilgrimage: A Spiritual and Cultural Journey*

Charles Foster takes us on a fascinating journey through diverse places and religious traditions in a search for an open Christian understanding of pilgrimage. In the process, he uncovers the manifold ways in which pilgrims explore worlds within themselves and beyond themselves—their inner journeys as well as their physical travels.

Prof. John Eade
CRONEM (Centre for Research on Nationalism,
Ethnicity and Multiculturalism
Southlands College, Roehampton University

ALSO BY CHARLES FOSTER

The Selfless Gene: Living with God and Darwin

The Jesus Inquest: The Case For—and
Against—the Resurrection of the Christ

Wired for God? The Biology of Spiritual Experience

Choosing Life, Choosing Death: The Tyranny
of Autonomy in Medical Ethics and Law

Tracking the Ark of the Covenant: By Camel, Foot,
and Ancient Ford in Search of Antiquity's Greatest Treasure

The Christmas Mystery: What on Earth Happened at Bethlehem?

www.charlesfoster.co.uk

THE SACRED JOURNEY

charles foster

THOMAS NELSON
Since 1798

NASHVILLE   DALLAS   MEXICO CITY   RIO DE JANEIRO

Published in Nashville, Tennessee, by Thomas Nelson. Thomas Nelson is a registered trademark of Thomas Nelson, Inc.

Thomas Nelson, Inc., titles may be purchased in bulk for educational, business, fund-raising, or sales promotional use. For information, please e-mail SpecialMarkets@ ThomasNelson.com.

Unless otherwise noted, Scripture quotations are taken from the NEW REVISED STANDARD VERSION BIBLE. © 1989, Division of Christian Education of the National Council of the Churches of Christ in the United States of America.

Scripture quotations marked NIV are from the HOLY BIBLE: NEW INTERNATIONAL VERSION®, © 1973, 1978, 1984 by International Bible Society. Used by permission of Zondervan Publishing House. All rights reserved.

ISBN 978-0-8499-4609-7 (trade paper)

Library of Congress Cataloging-in-Publication Data

Foster, Charles A., 1962–
  The sacred journey / Charles Foster.
    p. cm.
  Includes bibliographical references.
  ISBN 978-0-8499-0099-0 (hardcover)
  1. Christian pilgrims and pilgrimages. 2. Spiritual life—Christianity. I. Title.
  BV5067.F67 2010
  263'.041—dc22

                    2009053295

Printed in the United States of America

10 11 12 13 14 RRD 7 6 5 4 3 2 1

For David Monteath,
a great pilgrim who doesn't like to leave London

Go as a pilgrim and seek out danger . . .

JAMES ELROY FLECKER

Our interest's on the dangerous edge of things . . .

ROBERT BROWNING, "BISHOP BLOUGRAM'S APOLOGY"

CONTENTS

FOREWORD

In every listing of the seven ancient practices of our faith, pilgrimage always is the last to be named. There are two good reasons for that. One is organizational, and one is cautionary. Pilgrimage, you see, is the most dangerous of the seven.

When Christianity came up out of Judaism, it brought with it much of the prophecy and heritage and narrative that are the common or shared and generative grounding of both those faiths. Because for almost two centuries of the common era, the bulk of (or eventually just "many") Christians were Jewish by natal tradition, the distinctions we make today between the two communions was neither so clear nor even so popularly assumed as they are to us now. So it was that the seven ancient practices—or disciplines, as they once were called—came effortlessly out of Judaism into Christianity as the principal ways of forming or organizing the religious-specific or devout life.

Three of the seven—tithing, fasting, and the sacred meal—monitor or inform the physical body in space. The other four—fixed-hour prayer, the keeping of the Sabbath, the observance of the liturgical year, and pilgrimage—pace human life within the fourth dimension of time itself.

Tithing takes a set portion of the product of our bodies' labors and returns it in thanksgiving and as surtax to the One who enables our work and for whom and to whose glory that work is done. Fasting, of all human exercises, is the one that most completely allows us to withdraw for a set period from secular or external concerns and enter instead into total dependence upon God and without that most fundamental of human distractions, our need to eat. The sacred meal, be it the Passover or the Lord's Supper or the Mass or the Eucharist or even the *Id al Fahr*, allows us, by contrast, to move into the most complete form of union that a community of human beings can achieve—the sharing of the sensual and sustaining joy of eating together at a common table.

Fixed-hour prayer, which is often referred to as "keeping the hours" or "observing the daily offices," monitors the day. It calls Christians to stop every three hours and together, as the scattered but united Church on earth, to offer praise and honor to our God. The keeping of Sabbath paces the next largest unit of human time, the week. So likewise, observing the liturgical year paces an even larger increment of time, the year itself. In its observance, the faithful among us relive during every physical year the stories and salvation thrust of our heritage, thereby not only calling ourselves to more wondrous worship, but also teaching the faith to our young at a most intimate and natural level. All of that leaves pilgrimage.

The logistical reason, as I have said, for pilgrimage's coming last among the seven is that it monitors and focuses the largest unit of time. That is, it can be seen as monitoring or focusing the efforts and desires of a lifetime into one holy event; or it can be seen as a metaphor for a whole life's thrust toward union with God; or it can be understood as an infrequently recurring physical journeying of an increasing complexity, one that grows as the soul grows stronger and stronger and more and more earnest in its intentions. Regardless, however, of the frequency of its occurrence, pilgrimage is the one of the ancient seven that most threatens what is familiar and what has been . . . threatens them both with the almost absolute certainty that nothing will ever be the same again. The old verities will either die on pilgrimage or else they will rejuvenate and morph into sinewy understandings and holy affections that change every part of the life being lived. Either way, with pilgrimage, nothing is ever as it once was. Beware.

All of that said, I must now make confession. My confession is that we have been working for some four, almost five, years now on this series of books about the Seven Ancient Practices. Our work (and most certainly my part of it) has been driven by a fierce and unrelenting surety that while spiritual formation, for better or for worse, is an almost inevitable part of being human, Christian formation is not necessarily so; neither are the two the same.

Reformation Christianity, by which we Western Christians all—Protestant, Roman, and Orthodox alike—have to some greater or lesser extent been shaped, was keen on keeping tithing as a requirement of the faith. There was no question about that. Likewise, the keeping of the Sabbath was aggressively central to Christian formation. Post-Reformation, the observation of the Lord's Supper was to occur upon occasion, but not overmuch, lest folk find themselves slipping once more into the old Romanish ways of mass every Sabbath, with all its attendant candles and bells and vestments and rich chalices. And the matter of the liturgical year was to be tempered also. It was agreeable and reasonable to keep the major holy days of Christmas and Easter, but too many saints' days and lesser feasts distracted the attention and diffused one's focus from Christ to His disciples and, worst of all, to His later followers. As for fasting, Protestant theologians may be said only to have tipped their hats at it in passing, so to speak. But pilgrimage was different. As Charles Foster tells us in *The Sacred Journey*, "Martin Luther, a man never short on certainty, thundered that 'all pilgrimages should be stopped,'" and for good reason. Pilgrimage, whatever else it does, completely undoes certainty.

And thus my confession . . . my confession that as general editor in this series, I believed earnestly and prayerfully in the necessity of the work and its ordained purposes, but I did most truly dread the work on pilgrimage. In fact, I spent a goodly part of these last few editing years being grateful that pilgrimage was the last of the seven and, therefore, years (though eventually only months) away. Foolish me.

Indeed, in reading Charles Foster's words, from the very first draft of *The Sacred Journey* to the finished book you now have in your hand, all I could say to myself, over and over again, was exactly that: "Foolish me!" What you are now holding is, I suspect, as near a masterpiece of pilgrimage writing as we have ever seen. It certainly is, hands-down and far and away, the best book on pilgrimage I have ever seen.

Let there be no mistake, though. Foster pulls no punches. Every one of you who reads this book will find at least one thing you totally disagree with and a whole handful of those you want to question. Please do so. Otherwise, none of it is pilgrimage.

And one last word, in closing . . . if we read and do not do, we are told, then we have become like those who sit on the street corners, shouting to passersby to play for us and sing for us, but remaining unchanged by their songs . . . which is to say that I pray God will bless our tithes, our fasts, our communions, our hours, our Sabbaths and our years; but I today pray especially that He will bless our pilgrimages.

Phyllis Tickle

General Editor

The Ancient Practices Series

PREFACE

LOTS OF HUMANS WANDER. HISTORY IS CRISSCROSSED BY their tracks. Sometimes there are obvious reasons for wandering: to get better food for themselves or their animals; to escape weather, wars, or plague. But sometimes they do it—at great expense and risk—in the name of a supernatural being. This is very strange.

There are many books about pilgrimage: personal accounts, histories, sociological studies, and more or less structured anthologies of pilgrim tales and reflections. I have read quite a few of them. Many are superb. This book does not seek to compete with them. I am interested in three questions:

1. How did anyone ever think that a journey, such as a journey made by a barn swallow, had any religious significance?
2. Were they right?
3. If they were, what should we do with the insight?

I have tried to articulate a theology of pilgrimage. Some will be hurt and offended by it, and I'm sorry about that. It goes roughly like this:

A. Traveling is fundamental to the definition and the psyche of human beings. We can suppress the desire to move, but if we do, nasty things happen to our heads, our societies, our souls, and our coronary arteries.

B. Since earliest times there has been a bitter battle between settlers and nomads, portrayed, of course, in the story of Cain and Abel. Historicaly, Cain seems to have gotten the upper hand.

C. In the Judeo-Christian tradition, Yahweh is loudly and unequivocaly on the side of the nomads. He was a pilgrim God, traveling in a box slung over the shoulders of refugees and worshipped in a tent.

D. Yahweh's preference for the nomads is understandable. Yahweh, whenever and in whatever guise he appeared, was a traveler. There are things about the nomad's life that embody Yahweh's values and character: life on the edges; indiscriminate and costly hospitality; solidarity with the marginalized (most of the nomad's time is spent outside main centers and in the company of peripheral people); intimate relationships with humans and the environment; a new view at every step; the loosest possible hold on possessions. And although many nomadic societies are hierarchical, there's an inevitable democracy among travelers. When everyone walks, no one's a king and everyone's a king. But let's not get too romantic about the margin-people. They still need salvation. They're just likely to find it easier to grasp than center-people do. It's notoriously hard for poor little rich boys to enter the kingdom of heaven.

E. When Yahweh became a man, he was a homeless vagrant. He walked through Palestine proclaiming that a mysterious kingdom had arrived. That was and is the gospel. He called people to follow him, and that meant walking. The kingdom that sprang up around his dusty feet was weird: it was a place in which the first were last and the last were first. This Yahweh-man, partly because he was an itinerant tramp and partly because that's the way the kingdom always works, particularly fascinated the people on the edge of things: the underdogs, the despised. He wasn't a big hit with the urban establishment.

F. Being Christian (a word too contaminated by millennia of hypocrisy, violence, and downright error to be safe) *means following the Yahweh-man* and expanding the topsy-turvy kingdom movement (significant word, that).

G. Pilgrimage is wandering after God. That it may be to a definite destination doesn't mean that it's not wandering, and it doesn't destroy its continuity with the beloved nomads and the kingdom-preaching wanderings of Jesus.

H. There is a potent and important connection between the necessary, self-imposed marginalization of the pilgrim and Jesus' own bias toward the edge-people. Christian pilgrimage can and should be a walk with Jesus. And that is necessarily a walk in kingdom territory, under those upside-down kingdom rules. The pilgrim road is a physical peninsula of the kingdom. As the kingdom sprang up around the sandals of Jesus, so kingdom flowers can spring up around pilgrim boots. Not necessarily, of course, but it often happens.

I. Edges are exciting places. It is there that different things collide and, therefore, that new syntheses happen. Just think about Portuguese cookery. To mix pork and clams and make savory cakes is insane, but the world would be much poorer if it had not happened. And it could only happen on the wild edge of a sober continent.

J. Physical pilgrimage involves bodies, blisters, hunger, and diarrhea. And it's a kingdom activity. It is accordingly one of the best prophylactics against, and cures for, one of the deadliest and most prevalent diseases crippling the church: gnosticism. It is also effective against bigotry, self-righteousness, and angst.

K. Pilgrimage is a journey back. It can give us new eyes—the eyes of children. And that's just as well, because only those who come as children can enter that strange kingdom. Children's eyes see color and significance where we see only grays and emptiness. Pilgrims are dancing, delighting children. In the curious spiritual geometry of the kingdom, you can only go forward by going back.

L. Arrival is less important than the journey. This is because, if the journey is a walk with the Yahweh-man, there is an important sense in which you have arrived already. Yes, intimacy develops, but do you ever say of a relationship, "I've arrived"? Along the road there may be moments of epiphany, but if not, that's fine. Ecstasy isn't of the essence of relationship. But expect things to happen. Your incremental shuffle along the road is an incremental edging forward of kingdom borders—it's a restoration of broken things and a making of new things. The leopard might lie down with the lamb, but if anyone suggests that I'm saying if you go on pilgrimage you'll be able to talk to the birds, they haven't read the book properly.

M. There's nothing heretical about the idea of a particularly sacred place. Yes, there is a sense in which everything is sacred—the veil between the sacred and the secular has been ripped down. But that doesn't mean that sanctity doesn't bubble up particularly vigorously in certain places.

N. Not everyone can go on physical pilgrimage. But everyone can have the mind of the nomad-disciple. The lessons taught by the road need to be applied from birth to death.

O. Pilgrimage can give a taste of Christian radicalism. In fact "Christian radicalism" is a tautology: nothing that is not radical is Christian. That takes some grasping. The road can help us grasp it. A stockbroker on pilgrimage for a week will be able to imagine better what it means to leave everything and follow Jesus. He'll be on the fringes of places and the fringes of society, and hence in the heart of the kingdom and the company of its elite. For that week he'll be an ally of Abel, not an enemy. Those little tastes of the kingdom can be addictive.

P. Salvation is by grace, not by pilgrimage. But pilgrimage can help to create the conditions in which grace can work best.

Q. So get up and out and follow.

Pilgrimage is ubiquitous. But there is something particularly odd about Christian pilgrimage. I deal very briefly and blandly with the role of pilgrimage in other religions, and I quote a good deal from the pilgrim literature of other religions. Sometimes that is to illustrate how their ideas of pilgrimage differ from the Christian notion—often it is because they have important, beautiful, and significant things to say in their own right.

When I talk about pilgrimage, I generally have in mind the sort of journeys that characterized the Christian Middle Ages and have grown massively in popularity in recent decades: fairly long treks on foot, horseback, or these days by bicycle to one of the ancient pilgrimage centers, sleeping in pilgrim hostels, bunkhouses, tents, or ditches. Some people get a lot out of organized bus tours around religious sites, staying in hotels with their religious compatriots. I wouldn't, and I can't understand the appeal. That's no doubt a fault in me. I haven't written about those experiences because I've never had them.

Relics and indulgences: I don't see it as my job to defend everything about medieval pilgrimages. There were some grotesque and deadly abuses. But I do have a duty to suspend the instinctive Protestant horror I feel when a saint's bone or a plenary indulgence is mentioned, and ask what all that is about.

I should point out, before anyone else does, that in writing as I have done about the radical kingdom, I'm utterly hypocritical. I live in a house in Oxford, not a tent. I cycle to work, and I work in ancient, cloistered libraries. I am middle-class, middle-aged, and rather fat. So are most of my friends. I sometimes feel, smugly, that I've done my apprenticeship in the wilderness. But my hypocrisy doesn't mean that what I've written is wrong. It just means that I'm in desperate danger.

This book has been an exhilarating journey for me. Thank you for sharing it.

Charles Foster

Oxford, United Kingdom

ACKNOWLEDGMENTS

LITERALLY THOUSANDS OF PEOPLE SHOULD BE THANKED, notably the people I've traveled with and learned from. Most of them I've never spoken to, but I've pillaged their smiles, frowns, profundities, and absurdities; and I'm much the richer for it.

But I've spoken to some of my traveling companions, and to them I'm grateful for their patience and wisdom. Again I've robbed them. They include Mandy Murphy, Chris Beckingham, Keith Powell, Ian Jones, Pramod Kumar Joshi, David Peddie, Geoff Somers, Hette de Wette, Joan Crooks, Terence Grady, Jo Zias, Jonathan Brooke, David Monteath, Catharine De Rienzo, Lee Glassman, Esti Herskowitz, Chris Smith, Simon Heginbotham, Ishaq Salman, and Chris Thouless. And Tom.

Where I have cited conversations and incidents, I have generally changed the name of the actor, and often the nationality.

Just before I started to write this book, I met Shane Claiborne. There was the authentic prophetic voice, if ever I have heard it. He reminded me of the existence and urgency of the Sermon on the Mount. His talks have colored several passages in this book.

David Monteath read the whole manuscript in draft and made detailed and scarily pertinent comments. The book is a lot better for it.

James Orr sorted out my Latin.

Matt Baugher, Jennifer McNeil, and the team at Thomas

Nelson have been fantastic. This project was their idea, and it was a great privilege to be invited to write this book. For my introduction to Thomas Nelson I thank my peerless agent, Chip Macgregor. Mary Hollingsworth copyedited the manuscript and Amanda Hope Haley proofed it with great sensitivity, erudition, and care.

At the end of every set of acknowledgments, my wife, Mary, appears. I always apologize to her for all the absences, as if that makes it all right. I know that it doesn't. I hope this book might explain some of them better than I've been able to do so far.

PROLOGUE

1. Sometime in the late ninth century, big Atlantic breakers threw a small boat ashore on the rocky north coast of Cornwall. Three Irishmen staggered out, crossed themselves, and kissed the sand. A week before, taking food only for a week, they had set out from Ireland. Their boat had no oars—that would have been faithless. They got to Cornwall just in time. "They wanted to live in a state of pilgrimage for the love of God," the *Anglo-Saxon Chronicle* tells us. "They cared not where."

2. Sometime in the early twenty-first century, somewhere in the United States, a family was preparing to go to church. They dressed themselves in their best clothes. It was the father's big day. He was a local lawyer, and he had volunteered to coordinate the fund-raising drive. The church hoped to expand its premises and needed $5 million to do it. One of the fund-raising suggestions was to have a sponsored three-mile walk, and the father was going to sell the idea to the congregation. The family drove to church past the embarrassing shantytown that the police, despite the father's protestations, refused to dismantle. The father did his presentation, to thunderous applause, followed by

Bunyan's great hymn. "I'll fear not what men say," they sang lustily. "I'll labor night and day to be a pilgrim." The family then drove home, and over the turkey dinner planned the next Florida vacation.

3. Sue had multiple sclerosis (MS). It took her twenty minutes to crawl upstairs. She called the stairs "Mount Sinai," because it was there she had learned so much.

4. "I don't have Thomas's advantage," moaned Sam. "He could plunge his hand into the wounds of Christ. The best I can do is to go to the places where they say he walked, and see if the accounts in those old, strange New Testament books stack up. I fly to Tel Aviv tomorrow."

5. A young Hindu in New York gave up his job at a merchant bank and became a wandering *sannyasi*, pacing the roads with a begging bowl. His parents were distraught. "Why?" they asked. "We gave you all the advantages."

    "I am truly grateful," he said, "but I want to find life, and I know no other way to find it."

6. Victoria wanted to do the best thing for her husband, her children, and her community. She was uneasy when she read the Gospels but thought it not only irresponsible but also downright wrong to think of waltzing off to Jerusalem, Santiago, or the local homeless shelter, leaving someone else to cook, clean, and run the local Alpha course at church.

7. Andy was dying. He bought a boat, said good-bye to his friends, and sailed out into the Atlantic, intending never to return.

8. With a broken marriage behind her and a bleak, cat-filled spinsterhood ahead, Jane locked up her London house and started to walk to Rome. She had no orthodox religious belief, but she thought something might happen on the way.

   Which of these examples, if any, includes a pilgrim? Give reasons for your answer.

1

THE STRANGE STRIDER

Whereas most other mammalian bipeds hop or waddle, we stride. Homo sapiens is the only mammal that is adapted exclusively to bipedal striding.

—Encyclopedia Britannica

When man was first born, somewhere in East Africa, he began to walk. He was splendidly equipped to do so. He had long, straight hind limbs, bad for climbing trees but excellent for hoisting up his head so that he could get a long view across the savannah, and excellent for striding. He was called *Homo sapiens*—the thinking man—but he could equally well have been called *Homo ambulans*—the walking man. Indeed his thinking and his walking have been inextricably entwined.

He walked down the Nile and across the Sinai land bridge into Europe and Asia. Sometimes he stopped walking, and then there was disaster. But there have always been wanderers. They have stubbornly refused to settle, and from the edges of the settlements they have looked critically, pityingly, and prophetically in at the settlers. Their eyes have glinted menacingly in the night. The settlers have felt threatened, inadequate, and judged, and they have responded in the way that all fat bullies react—by violence. Wanderers have been denounced and hunted, but never humiliated.

In the Abrahamic religious tradition, God makes no secret of his clear bias for the wanderer. He is on the side of the Bedouin and loathes the city. It is not surprising. Abraham, the father of Judaism, Christianity, and Islam, was the archetypal desert Bedouin. Jesus was homeless: "Foxes have holes, and birds of the air have nests; but the Son of Man has nowhere to lay his head," he declared, and with pride, not regret.[1] "I'm in the line of that vagrant, Abraham," he was saying. The prophet Mohammed denounced the evils of the suburbs. Islam is a religion of black goat-hair tents, withering sun, and sandstorm. Religion, like everything else, tends to go bad when it is imported to the town.

Humans have never forgotten that they were designed as walkers. When things go wrong, they go for a walk, and whether through the action of serotonin or some ancient metaphysical mechanics, that seems to make things better. When they want to feel what it is like to be a human being (instead of a lawyer, an academic, or an acronym), they lace up their boots. When they want to feel even more human, they take off their boots and walk barefoot. When they want to describe the human's strange relationship with time, they use the language of the road: "Time is marching on"; "Stop dragging your feet"; "I think she's coming to the end of the road."

All the great religions have acknowledged this fundamental relationship between the man, his feet, and his place in the universe. The acknowledgment has taken many forms. One of them is pilgrimage. It is unstoppable. In the Middle Ages, huge economies were built on it. They still are. Each year about 3 million Muslims make the Hajj, 5 million Christians go to Lourdes, 20 million Hindus visit the 1,800 sacred sites in India, and about 700,000 devotees trundle reverently to Graceland, the shrine of Elvis Presley in Memphis, Tennessee. As conventional churchgoing plummets, the number of people taking to the road rises. These are good times to buy shares in companies owning hotels in Santiago de Compostela. If you think Christianity is all about signing up to a set of doctrinal propositions, that will worry you sick. "Now the LORD said to Abram, 'Go from your country and your kindred and your father's house to the land that I will show you' . . . So Abram went."[2] And ever since, men have been going to the lands they think God is showing them.

Judaism was forged on the march, in the wind and blazing sun of Sinai. "You're a pilgrim people," said God, "and don't you forget it." And so to help them remember, he stuck walks into their liturgical calendar. "Three times in the year all your males shall appear before the LORD God, the God of Israel."[3] That wasn't just putting on your best clothes and going to the synagogue around the corner. Unless you lived wherever the tabernacle was, that meant taking to the road for

Passover, *Shau'ot*, and *Sukkot*. It meant dust, expense, disease, and bedbugs.

As does the Islamic Haj. Between the eighth and the thirteenth days of the twelfth month, Saudi Arabia's population swells massively. Charter flights, bought with the life savings of Pakistani peasants and shopkeepers, clog the skies. Trucks, axle-bendingly overloaded, cut into the liquid tarmac on the road to Mecca. Boats shudder across the Red Sea; the pilgrims shave their heads and throw the hair into the wash from the engines. "Pilgrimage to the House," says the Qur'an, "is a duty laid upon people which they owe to Allah, those of them that can afford the journey thither."[4] The *House*, here, is the "House of God"—the Ka'aba in Mecca, believed by Muslims to have been built by Abraham and Ishmael. It was an important shrine long before the birth of Islam, and it contains fragments of the black stone (perhaps a meteorite) once kissed by the prophet Mohammed.

The Prophet's great campaign was against polytheism, and so a centralization of the faith was crucial. If you sanctioned little local shrines, there would be a danger of breeding little local gods, little local cults, and little local heresies.[5] The Hajj—the mandatory pilgrimage to the one Mecca—reminds Muslims that there is one God, Allah; that he spoke very specifically to one man, the Prophet, in this place; that there is only one true revolution against unbelief, this one. It is an invigorating reminder of the internationality and scale of Islam, a return to the Abrahamic routes and roots, and a reminder that stasis kills. "You're just passing through," says the Hajj. "Keep moving. Neither Dhaka nor Jakarta's your real home. Neither, in fact, is Mecca. You are built for Paradise. Walk on." And when they get to the Ka'aba, that's what they do. They keep circling, seven times in all, following in the wing beats of the angels that circle the throne of Allah (for even the angels are travelers).

And when the pilgrims have done that, there's more traveling. They run between two hills to remember Hagar, Ishmael's mother, and go to the Mount of Mercy, where the Prophet spoke to his followers for the last time before his death. The connection with Abraham is reforged during the Feast of Eid ul-Adha (which remembers Abraham's sacrifice of a ram instead of his son), when a sacrificed animal is eaten—a desert meal, commemorating a desert man.

The journey to Mecca used to be dangerous and arduous. It sometimes still is. But Islam is clear: the journey itself forms no part of the Hajj. The Hajj proper begins when the pilgrim reaches Mecca. This dictate is a useful bulwark against heresy. If the point of the Hajj is to promote doctrinal unity and purity, it is wise to say that the only legitimate experiences are those that occur under the umbrellas of tradition and clerical supervision. The road is an unpredictable, epiphanic place. Things happen to people there. When you step onto the road, you throw open the experiential floodgates. And who knows what might come in?

That isn't a worry that tortures Hindu and Buddhist wanderers. They want to be transformed by the land, and they are. The tradition of pilgrimage in Hinduism and Buddhism is vertiginously ancient. The Mahabharata (c. 400 BC), one of the foundational documents of Hinduism, lists many pilgrimage sites; Buddhism has a well-established circuit by the third century BC at the very latest.

Hinduism sees the land as expressly sacred. There are various ways of trying to express that sanctity, but one of the commonest is to see India as the body of a goddess, mythically dismembered and scattered between the coral seas. Her body permeates, fertilizes, and sanctifies India. A holy mountain might be her nipple; a cave might be her navel. In the forest, as you are waiting to die, you might hear her heartbeat trembling through the earth.

The physical form of the landscape is therefore supremely important. A landslide that sheers the face off a hill might be the tears rolling down the goddess's cheeks. The landscape dictates religious practice: it is not a theater in which religion happens. When a new temple to Vishnu was recently built near Birmingham, UK, it was an exact replica of the Vishnu temple at Tirupati in Andhra Pradesh and, crucially, the seven hills in which the original temple nestles were faithfully reproduced.

Pilgrims roll like waves across India, crashing as surf against the beaches of Varanasi, Vrindavan, and Badrinath at the great festivals. Some pilgrims ride the waves all their lives, begging for their food, the calluses on the soles of their feet about as thick as their ankles.

Even when the software engineers from Bangalore come to a holy place in their air-conditioned limousines, they still have to walk. They waddle in tight terylene trousers along prescribed processional routes. Buildings are not for congregation, shelter, or interest: they exist to be walked through.

And then there is Christianity.

Jesus was a *very* Jewish Palestinian. The Christians believed he was God—that God had burst uniquely into space and time and wandered around the Holy Land. The physical evidence in Palestine had an apologetic importance for Christianity that no similar evidence had in any other religion, and the theology of the incarnation lent that evidence a devotional power that not even the fingernails of the Buddha had for Buddhists. The accounts of Jesus' life are geographically very explicit. He had said, "Follow me." Many took him literally.

Pilgrimage to the Holy Land was difficult until the rise of Constantine,[6] but thereafter, for a while, it was both facilitated and popularized by the efforts of the formidable Helena, Constantine's mother, who trawled the Near East for biblical sites, slapping on labels that by and large have stuck. Some of her identifications are almost certainly wrong (Mount Sinai, for instance); some have survived more or less unscathed the worst that modern archaeological skepticism can throw at them (the Church of the Holy Sepulchre in Jerusalem, for example, which contains the alleged sites of the death and resurrection of Jesus); many will forever bear the verdict "not impossible" (such as the Church of the Nativity in Bethlehem). It was Helena who drew the pilgrims' map of the Holy Land.

Her map was soon encrusted with legend and theology. The Church of the Holy Sepulchre was thought to be the place where Adam was created and where Abraham lifted the knife to kill Isaac. (In Jewish thought, both happened on the Temple Mount.) If you go to the Church of the Holy Sepulchre today and can fight your way through the melee, you will see a crack in the rock of Golgotha. All the tour groups are told that the crack appeared at the death of Jesus: "The earth shook, and the rocks were split."[7] The Catholic and Orthodox tour groups are then told that the blood of Jesus flowed through the crack to the grave of Adam below. The first Adam was thus redeemed by the blood of the second "Adam."

From the fourth century, pilgrim guidebooks were a commercial hit. We meet some of them later. They tell us a lot about how myths are made. Humans are desperate to see their vital abstractions made concrete, and the heat of the Holy Land crystallizes abstractions beautifully. The devout mind poured the blood of Christ into the great lamp that hung in the middle of the Dome of the Rock, and linked a cistern near the Dome with Ezekiel's prophecy about water coming forth from the temple.[8] There is also straightforward competition with the rival religions. Islam says that the footprint of the Prophet's horse, Buraq, is visible in the Dome of the Rock. Christian pilgrims, not to be outdone, saw Christ's footprints there, connected with one of his visits to the Temple.

In AD 638 the armies of Islam swept up from Arabia and took Jerusalem. The shock and the shame reverberated throughout Christendom and indeed acted as an adhesive, sticking together its disparate parts. Christians loathed one another, but they hated the Muslim conquerors of Jerusalem even more. Christian pilgrimage shuddered to a near halt. A few intrepid travelers still made it there, but they were probably more daring than devoted.

The Christian world fulminated and plotted, but life went on. You can't stop caribou or swallows from migrating, and the pilgrim instinct could not be suppressed. So local shrines blossomed (those with relics from the Holy Land doing particularly well); the tombs of saints attracted more attention than ever.

In an ecstasy of bloodlust fueled by guilt, fear, and apocalyptic hymns, Jerusalem was stormed by the self-styled "armed pilgrims" of the first crusade in 1099. After the guts had been hosed down the drains of the Temple Mount, a strange kingdom started to rule the Holy Land. This was a kingdom of men in steel, wearing hair shirts—men a long way from home who had seen and done terrible things, men for whom time was short and redemption urgent.

Their energy was astonishing. Realizing their supply lines were dangerously long, they built a chain of castles to guard them. Those castles, built in the most straitened circumstances, are some of the great architectural glories of the Middle Ages. It was sweating on the battlements of the summit of the Krak des Chevaliers, in the Syrian highlands, that I first admired anything made by men. Whenever I am in Jerusalem, I sleep in a crusader cellar. And each night, when the cameras have stopped flashing and the coaches have belched away to Tel Aviv, I go to the Church of the Holy Sepulchre, the best thing the crusaders ever did or tried to do, and sit at Calvary, breathing old frankincense in the dark.

The brutal, dreaming kingdom of Jerusalem didn't last a hundred years. In 1187 the crusaders marched out onto the fields of Hattin in the Galilee to meet the army of Saladin. They carried with them the most precious relic of all—the True Cross, discovered by Helena in a cave under the Holy Sepulchre. They thought they couldn't lose. The Cross had defeated the powers of darkness and routed Satan; what chance did an Ayyubid upstart have?

But this time it was the crusaders who were routed. The

Cross was carried off in triumph by the cheering hordes of Islam and has never been seen again. The disaster of Hattin was both military and theological. The kingdom was broken. Jerusalem fell shortly afterward. This should have prompted an agonized reassessment of the *raison d'etre* of crusading. There was certainly plenty of agonizing. The instrument of salvation had gone. Had salvation gone with it? Had God definitively withdrawn his favor from his crusading *mujahidin*? Was Islam right in saying that it had superseded Christianity? Hattin injected doubt deep into the psyche of the Christian West.

But on one level it did not take the crusaders or Christendom long to get over their spasm of introspection. God, they decided, with the help of a lot of Old Testament footnotes, had judged them for their faithlessness, their immorality, their arrogance. But not their violence. And how should they repent and regain his favor? By redoubling their armed efforts. By avenging the sleight to the name of God that had been uttered at Hattin. God was like them: his honor was everything.

And so the crusades grumbled bloodily on. Each wave contained men who saw themselves as pilgrims, often with a primarily penitential objective. And although the politics of the papacy increasingly wrote the real agenda of the crusaders, protection of pilgrim traffic to the Holy Land featured strongly in the rhetoric of the crusade preachers.

No subsequent crusade achieved anything like the success of the first. In their frustration, later armed pilgrims flung themselves on Jews and Christians. Christian Constantinople was sacked by the fourth crusade in 1204, massively boosting the relics trade in Europe and therefore increasing the number of European pilgrimage destinations. But Jerusalem itself remained in Islamic hands until British commander Edmund Allenby, dismounting from his horse in deference to the Holy City, entered it on foot in 1917 after defeating the Ottomans. "Today the Crusades have ended," he said, unwisely.

The Middle Ages were the heyday of pilgrimage. Although the crusades made things tense, there was always some traffic to Jerusalem. The "Saracens" (as the occupiers of the Holy Land tended to be called generically) made life difficult, irritating, and expensive for pilgrims, but the real dangers came from bandits, storm, and plague. Undeterred, Venetian travel agents put together arduous package tours to the Holy Land; early backpackers made their own way there.

The pilgrims' motives were as mixed as those of modern travelers. Most had some sort of devotional interest; many were working off the guilt of adultery or murder; some believed they would leave their lameness or their leprosy there; some were relic-hunters, out to make a fortune from saints' teeth, prophets' hair, and chippings from the pillar of the scourging; some were adventurers, bored with the constraints of medieval life, in which one could often live a long life without going outside the parish. And some, as insecure as St. Thomas was and I am, hoped that their faith would be increased if they put their fingers in the marks left by Jesus.

Jerusalem was always the preeminent Christian pilgrimage destination, distinguished by its biblical significance and the sheer difficulty of getting there. But it was followed closely by Rome (the seat of Peter's successors, the site of the tombs of Peter and Paul, and cluttered with looted relics) and Santiago de Compostela (said to contain the bones of St. James the Apostle, allegedly translocated there miraculously after his AD 44 martyrdom and said to have been discovered in Galicia in northwest Spain in 835).

In the second division, and the beneficiaries of international conflict, were the smaller shrines, such as England's Walsingham (containing a replica of the house in Nazareth where the Annunciation occurred, built according to plans disclosed in 1061 to a Saxon noblewoman, Richeldis, in the course of a vision of the Virgin Mary); and Canterbury, also in England, which established its miracle-working credentials almost immediately after the top of Archbishop Thomas à Becket's head was sliced off in the cathedral sanctuary by Henry II's knights in 1170. By the time Thomas was canonized three years later, Canterbury's merchants and hoteliers were already much fatter.

Then there had always been the little local shrines, often venerated in pre-Christian days and baptized by the Christians: sacred springs and pools; gravid mother-goddesses in sandstone, rechristened as the Virgin; trees fed with the blood of children and rebranded as sunshades for church picnics.

The Protestant Reformers by and large disapproved of pilgrimage and disapproved violently. They frowned at the cult of relics; they railed against the indulgences often associated with visits to pilgrimage sites; they thought the whole business was paralyzingly superstitious and fed the heresy that you could work out your own salvation. And so, as far as they could, they shut it down.

They were fairly successful for a while in the European Reformation countries. Those Canterbury entrepreneurs tightened their belts. English pilgrims no longer went in large numbers to Santiago.

It is easy to be misleadingly Eurocentric. Europe is not Christendom. Christianity is an Eastern religion that has had the misfortune to be particularly popular in the West (where its chances of being understood were lowest).

Outside the jurisdiction of the popes and the Reformers, pilgrimage has continued more or less unruffled by the squabbles of Europe. Orthodox Christians have continued to go faithfully to the tombs of their saints and the caves and pillars of their hermits. In India a shrine might be holy both because it is the knee of the Hindu goddess Sati, and because it is where a Portuguese missionary went screaming into eternity. There is quite enough holiness in India to go around—no one need feel jealous. And, with a few dishonorable and fairly recent exceptions, they haven't.

The Celts have generally plowed their own furrow in the sea, with only the most technical nod to Rome. The early Irish church, which blossomed within a century of St. Patrick's death in AD 462, recognized three types of martyrdom: "Red martyrdom," which was dying for Christ; "Green martyrdom," which involved strenuous ascetic practice; and "White martyrdom," which involved living years away from home. Irish pilgrims were both Green and White. The Greens might walk the snowy roads barefoot, remembering that Jesus' feet bled too. The White martyrs might follow the path of the gull or find their Jerusalem in a stone cell, looking out at the seals resting on the wrack.

The Reformers lost the war against pilgrimage. You can't root out something so fundamental to human identity. Christians of all denominations and none, and people with nothing other than the compulsion to walk, flock to Taizé, Santiago, Rome, and Jerusalem. Their motives are perhaps more mixed, or less well defined, than some of those medieval pilgrims. Many would say that they are going to find "themselves," or "what it's all about." If the New Testament theology of the kingdom is right, they might not be as self-indulgent or as heretical as Martin Luther would have thought they were.

Not everyone finds what he is looking for, but everyone finds something that he didn't have before and that he needs and wants. Pilgrimage involves doing something with whatever faith you have. And faith, like muscle, likes being worked.

In the Armenian chapel in the Church of the Holy Sepulchre, third-century pilgrims,[9] who must have battled their way there through hardships unimaginable to our pampered generation, drew a boat. It bears the inscription *Domine ivimus*: "Lord, we came."[10] And that's more than can be said for most.

2

THE KINGDOM ROAD: A THEOLOGY FOR WALKERS

[To] Be good news in all we do . . .
Is to walk as Jesus walked.

—Martyn Layzell [1]

"Aslan is on the move. The Witch's magic is weakening. . . ." Edmund
could at last listen to the other noise properly. A strange, sweet, rustling,
chattering noise. . . . It was the noise of running water. . . . And his heart
gave a great leap (though he hardly knew why) when he realized that the
frost was over. . . . And now the snow was really melting in earnest and
patches of green grass were beginning to appear in every direction.[2]

—C. S. Lewis

This is supposed to be a Christian book. It would have
been convenient if I had been able to illustrate the heart of
quintessentially Christian pilgrimage simply by putting deep,
moving Christian quotes alongside deep, moving Hindu,
Buddhist, Communist, Islamic, Parsi, and Jewish quotes and
saying, "There you are: Christians go for those reasons; the

others go for these. And Christians get X out of it; the others get Y and Z." But it can't be done. For every resonant, helpful, poetic, and theologically impeccable quote from a Christian source, there are dozens from the others.

I did a trial at my pastorate at Holy Trinity Brompton. Without indicating the source, I wrote down several dozen quotations on the subject of pilgrimage culled from most of the main religions. I asked the theologically sophisticated Christian audience to identify the "Christian" ones. They couldn't. They were hopeless. When I told them which was which, they were amused and horrified. A rather intense girl had identified a sixth-century Hindu text as "oozing the spirit of Jesus." (And who am I to say she was wrong?) Another said, ecstatically, that a poem was "one of the loveliest things I have ever read. I will use it every morning in my quiet time." Why, I wonder, should she have been dissuaded simply because it was one of the pearls of Islamic Persia?

So are there any differences between Christian and other pilgrimages? Two things emerge clearly from the accounts. First, the *journey* matters to the Christians. It's not all about *arrival.* And second (and no doubt related to this), the Christians by and large seem to have a lot more *fun.* Of course there are lots of pale, po-faced, pursed-lipped, tut-tutting, self-excoriating, life-denying, metaphorically black-suited Christian pilgrims. We will walk some of the way with some of them. And of course there are many jolly Hindus and Muslims. But taken as a whole, there are many more laughs on the Christian pilgrimages. The *typical* Christian pilgrim band is Chaucer's: bibulous, belching, pranking, sentimental, uncertain, tolerant, flawed, inconsistent, volatile, sympathetic, and fascinating. Better an evening in the Tabard Inn than a day with the hysterical fifteenth-century pilgrim Margery Kempe, weeping wildly in the Church of the Holy Sepulchre as she remembered the wounds of Christ.

This difference is important. And its roots are theological. We need to trace those roots before coming back to the trail. I think that the distinctive color, taste, variety, and vibrancy of the Christian pilgrims were direct consequences of their Christianity. And their Christianity was, as all real Christianity is, characterized by its uncompromising rejection of gnosticism. There's another reason why we need to talk about this. Pilgrimage, done properly, is one of the best-known antidotes to gnosticism. Gnosticism runs screaming at the sight of a muddy boot. When wise men prescribe pilgrimage, there's a fair chance that the diagnosis on the notes is "gnostic."

Gnosticism says that there are two opposing forces in the world: good and bad. The good forces are "spiritual"; the bad are corporeal. For a gnostic, being a good person involves rejecting the earthly and being "spiritual." Gnostics couldn't accept that Jesus was human: his humanity was an illusion. He was pure spirit, and pure spirit wouldn't dirty its incorporeal hands with flesh or dust.

The early church saw where all this led. It fought for its very life against Gnosticism, asserting that matter matters; that the incarnation is God's resounding yes to the material; that Jesus' appearance in the dust of Palestine during the reign of Caesar Augustus baptizes both time itself and the way humans process through it; that the ripping of the temple veil abolished the distinction between the sacred and the secular; that the unique doctrine of the resurrection of the *body* means that the coming kingdom will be a place that is experienced in a bodily way; that there is a crucial continuity between this world and the coming kingdom; that God hasn't given up on this world—he's not simply going to sling it in the fire and start again. In short, laughing, mourning, caring, walking along roads, and making love are sacramental activities. They can be building blocks of the kingdom. Eat, drink, and be merry, for tomorrow you *don't* die. Or the day after.

History says that the church won. I'm afraid I disagree. The battle is still raging. And it's not looking good for the church.

This morning a good Christian friend sent me an SMS text: "Spiritual (i.e., anything but this life), that's what I crave. Where's it to be (really) found?"

At church on Sunday we sang a song: "You're all I want. You're all I've ever needed."[3] But it wasn't true. It stuck in my throat. I want, and God wants me to want, lots of things apart from him: mountains, waves, and friends, for instance. And I need lots of things apart from him, too: food, air, and a functioning myocardium, for example. If it meant "Everything I want has its source, ultimately, in God," then that's fair enough, but that is a very, very different proposition, and it wasn't what most of the ecstatic but uncritical worshippers meant, or were trying to mean.

The song was followed by a hymn: "Naught be all else to me, save that thou art."[4] "Naught?" Is that really what God wants me to think? My wife? My children? The suffering millions? The fate of the snow leopard?

My friend, the song and the hymn were articulating a straightforward gnosticism. It is the ruling force in many modern churches. And the more devout and enthusiastic the church, the more in thrall to gnosticism it often is.

Gnosticism's grip is shown by the language we use when complimenting a Christian. "She's a really spiritual person," we say, meaning that she's a close follower of Jesus. But the biblically accurate compliment would be, "She's a well-mixed cocktail of mind, body, and spirit, infused with the Holy Spirit himself." And only well-mixed cocktails are fun at parties. Nobody looked at Margery Kempe and said, "Now there is life in all its fullness."

Last night I sat down and watched again a lecture by the famous mythologist Joseph Campbell. It was a splendid survey of the myths underpinning the world's great religions. It struck me again how very, very odd Christianity is. Its uniqueness lies in its relationship with a person—a person who felt time flowing as we do; who ate lamb chops and drank wine; who sometimes had a painfully full bladder; who cared enough about bodies to heal wherever he went and to change water into wine (and good wine, at that) to make the party wild; who was, as we will see, a fanatical walker. Any of the other religions will talk to you beautifully about spiritual things, and they will all (Judaism only equivocally, which is important) promise you some sort of ethereal, disembodied future. They all (with the exception, again, of most strands of Judaism) see our existence as a gnostic war of flesh and spirit. Suppress the flesh, they cry, and if you do it well enough, you will float on a cloud forever/become a drop of water in the sea of Nirvana/take your pick of the paradisal virgins (now, there's an irony). If Christianity isn't virulently anti-gnostic, it's not distinctive at all. Those church fathers were right to be worried.

Yet gnosticism is everywhere. If a movie is ever made about the church in the early twenty-first century, it should be called *Invasion of the Body Haters*. If pilgrimage is Christian at all, the pilgrims will grind gnosticism underfoot.

How did we get things so wrong? These aren't theological subtleties. But there is much worse to come.

"Come and follow Jesus," shouted the street-corner preacher. But where will that take me? What can I expect? What does it mean?[5]

Because I'm insecure, I like to ask people questions in the hope that they will agree with me. But sometimes it backfires badly.

I had been reading and rereading the Gospels. I photocopied them, put them in a ring binder, and went through them with a highlighter pen and a bundle of Post-It notes. My brow furrowed.

That evening we were having a big group of Christian friends over for dinner. They were from several denominations: a couple of pretty conservative evangelicals, a sprinkling of charismatics, a gentle Baptist, an Anglican as high as they come, and a brace of Catholics. Over the soup I said, "We're all agreed that we need to preach the gospel." The high Anglican shifted uncomfortably in his seat; the others nodded, spoon to mouth. "But what *is* the gospel?" I asked.

Only the conservative evangelicals looked confident and eager to answer. They were like greyhounds that had spotted a hare. One of them began; the other added footnotes, sometimes in the form of Bible references.

The gospel, they patiently and pityingly explained, was "the power of God for salvation to everyone who has faith, to the Jew first and also to the Greek."[6] It required an explicit acknowledgment of the sinner's unworthiness to enter the presence of God, for "all have sinned and fall short of the glory of God."[7] It required the sinner to put his trust in Jesus, who had died in our place once for all upon the cross, taking our sins upon him. That meant that we were clean in the eyes of God, and the anger that a righteous God necessarily feels towards sin falls on Jesus, not on us. Accordingly, when we die, we can go to be with God. "And indeed," added one of the charismatics, "we begin a new relationship with him now, through the power of the Holy Spirit."

"Quite," said the conservative, a little put out to have been interrupted, "but the main point to note [he looked over the bread rolls at the Catholics] is that salvation has nothing whatever to do with anything we do. Salvation is a gift that comes by grace; we receive it by faith and faith alone." He sank back in his seat, the good fight fought.

Well, the debate raged for a while, but nobody dissented significantly from this formula. Caveats were inserted, hairs were split, historical hypocrisies were revived, and I sat glumly at the table, wondering if I had completely missed the plot.

The plot I had been reading that afternoon was very different. Jesus is a man obsessed. He's a single-message man. He walks umpteen hundred miles in appalling conditions, shouting to anyone who will listen: "The kingdom of heaven has come near,"[8] and demonstrating it. That's the good news. Yes, he spells out the corollary, but it is terrifyingly simple. It's just, "Follow me."

You will struggle to find in the Gospels anything obviously analogous to "conversion."[9] One moment people are fishing, and the next they are following Jesus. They come, just as they are. They are immediately disciples. They start the journey. They don't pray the conversion prayer, come along to church for a bit, and then do a discipleship course. Sure, there's baptism, and Jesus endorses John's formula of repentance, and those are obviously crucial. But their relationship to the Jesus-following is never clear. It seems that unbaptized people were Jesus-followers. It is clear that Jesus-fascination often led to Jesus-following. It's still the case. We see it all the time, despite the obstacles to Jesus-fascination and Jesus-following that we put in people's way. I have known many, many people who have become entranced by Jesus and started to walk after him, desperate for more of his company. They haven't "repented" in the classical, explicit, formulaic way. They continue for a while to live lifestyles that would etch deep frowns into many in the church. But the longer they walk the road with Jesus, the more inevitable and complete repentance becomes. His presence has an antiseptic quality. They are baptized in the perfume that envelops him. For people who do physical pilgrimages, and for those first, itinerant apostles, the very act of starting to walk is inevitably a kind of repentance. They left their old lives behind and walked in the Jesus-direction.

The fascination and the following increased after Jesus' death and resurrection. Acts (Luke Part Two) tells us that "day by day the Lord added to their number those who were being saved."[10] The tense ("were being saved") is interesting and often abused. Here's my paraphrase: "Day by day the Lord increased the numbers of those who started their walk with him. He watched lovingly while they packed their bags, and then took them by the hand. They set out on the road together." Every conversion story in the New Testament is a launch party for a new travel book.

This kingdom Jesus talks about is a weird place. Its values are all back to front and upside down. The weak are the strong; the first are the last; the rich are destitute; the greatest are the least; if someone hits you, you say, "I love you; again, please." The disciples aren't chosen because of their theological understanding. They understand almost nothing except that Jesus is fascinating. He says, "Come," and they come. No Bible school, no doctrinal statement. They have an almost unerring instinct for the wrong end of the doctrinal stick.[11] During their time as disciples, they would never have been invited to speak at the Oxford University Intercollegiate Christian Union. The kingdom is an eternal party, and it has already started. Everyone's invited, but almost nobody comes. It's perhaps not surprising. We're told that if you come, you're likely to be killed. But who cares? If you get killed for dancing, you'll just carry on dancing forever.

How do you know that you're part of the party? Oh, you'll know. But there will come a time when the credentials are checked. And that's the scariest thing of all. It's not, apparently, a check of your theological orthodoxy. It's not a look at whether you have assented to certain propositions. That's not surprising. Even the demons believe.[12] Belief evidently matters because it somehow changes the sort of people we are and our consequent salvageability.[13] But all the same, I'm disappointed with God for having undervalued the importance of right doctrine. I reckon I'd do pretty well in an examination like that. But no, the test is whether I fed the hungry (aka Jesus) and visited Jesus (aka the neighborhood rapist) in prison.[14] It's queasy reading for someone like me, who has boomed pharisaically away over the years, denouncing as flabby, anemic, and un-Christian the dictates of the despised "social gospel." The message here is: unless you're despised, you've got things badly wrong; watch your back.

I presume that Jesus meant this stuff. I presume that when he said, "The first will be last," he meant it to be seriously bad news for the first. And so I wonder why I spend most of my time trying to be first. If he's right, then it's not just silly; it's downright deadly. And I presume that his clear preference for the outsiders, the people on the edges, means that he looks with deep suspicion at supposedly Christian states and institutions. Indeed at the whole anti-nomadic notion of the Christian Establishment. There aren't many modern economies that organize their international trade on the principle that, if someone asks for your shirt, you give him your coat as well. There aren't many politicians who say to their opponents, "You got fewer votes than I did, so you take the seat." As soon as someone is at the top, or at the center, they're being disobedient. If Jesus is right, the conversion of Constantine and the consequent Christianization of the Roman Empire were unmitigated catastrophes. Constantine made Christianity comfortable with worldly power, and a Christianity comfortable with worldly power isn't Christianity at all. If Jesus is right, we need to look askance at institutions. If this sounds like anarchy, that's because it is. But it's a kind, holy anarchy that would never plant a bomb.

We are always asking Jesus to be realistic, reminding him that we live in the real world and don't have the luxury, as he did, of being able to wander luggage-free around the world. To which he replies, "Why not come? I never said it would be easy. Few will find the road." We are always giving him little lessons in politics, economics, and pragmatism. "This system you appear to be criticizing, Jesus, is actually a good one, if you look at it properly. If this system collapses, the poor and downtrodden about whom you care so much will be the primary casualties." And he replies, "Try my system instead. Few ever have."

And that, broadly, was the rant to which I treated those dinner guests.

They looked at me strangely. The conservatives muttered something about Paul being pretty keen on theological correctness. The Catholics graciously pointed out that institutions were simply a reflection of Christianity's success, and I couldn't regret that, could I? The charismatics opened another bottle. But the Baptist, who had said nothing so far, said quietly, "Isn't the gospel an invitation to go for a walk with Jesus?"

Well, in a way, the conservatives agreed. But there was a lot more to it than that. The high Anglican looked embarrassed. But she was right. "Come, follow me," Jesus had said.

"That's what I did when I walked to Santiago," said the Baptist girl, and she described how, when her heart had been broken, she had put a Bible, a T-shirt, two pairs of pants, and a big box of Cuban cigarillos into her knapsack, caught the train to Paris, gone to High Mass in Notre Dame, and then started to walk along the old pilgrim route to Santiago de Compostela in Galicia. She walked for three months. The cigarillos had gone by the time she hit the Pyrenees, but by then she didn't need them. By the time she got to the Spanish border, she had a Swiss boyfriend, diarrhea, an invitation to a kibbutz in the Galilee, a deep suspicion of organized religion, worms, a shifting entourage of disciples from sixteen to seventy-nine and from nine countries, and an immovable conviction that she wanted to spend the rest of her life following Jesus. "It was as if the road were part of the kingdom," she said. "We sang as we went along, but if we didn't, the stones themselves would have sung." They had nothing and gave everything away, not out of some selfish belief that God would reward them if they did, but because "that's just how it worked." "If we met someone on the road, we scooped them up, and they came along with us. We didn't care what they'd done or what they believed. We were all going to the same place, and that was enough. If they were sick, we prayed for them, and they got better. The worms were immune to prayer, sadly." Usually they found somewhere to stay, but if not, they slept in woods and ditches, which trebled the fun. They tried to avoid the towns. "It felt wrong to be surrounded by walls—to be at the hub of anything. We were there because we wanted to be on the edge of things. Only then could we know what it was like to be cold-shouldered by the world. And do you know, there is a freedom at the edges that you never feel at the center? You can feel the wind in your face and get the long view. The walls of banks and shops block the wind, and you see only the wall. But most of all, he is there at the edges. Just as he had said he would be." She never got to Santiago. She didn't want to. The journey was enough.

The dinner guests didn't contradict her. We moved on to profiteroles and the Sudanese famine.

The physical pilgrim road can be an out-pouching of the kingdom. Imagine the kingdom as a city, the destination. There are various possible approach roads. The laws and many of the benefits of the kingdom extend along each of the roads. From the moment a traveler sets foot on the road with pilgrim intent, he is under a new jurisdiction. If he loses that intent, the road on which he walks becomes the ordinary Spanish, Roman, or Israeli tarmac.

The physical pilgrim has a number of advantages over the metaphorical pilgrim. He necessarily travels light, unless he is foolish enough to go in a car. He will find that he doesn't need as much as he thought he did. His ties with the tedious fripperies of life will loosen, and he will learn new pleasures—the pleasures of relationship, of rain, of conversation, of silence, of exhaustion. Simple food will have a taste that he could never have dreamed of in his Burger King days. Soon gnosticism will seem ridiculous. It is hard to believe that the only important thing about you is your spirit when you are straining in the bushes with amoebic dysentery, or if you eat the cheese at a farm I know in the anti-Lebanon range.

For the pilgrim, to pass a beggar by is not the unthinking prudence that it is in the city—it is to miss out on a friend. The pilgrim will be given new eyes for the suffering. He'll see a limp in a passerby that he wouldn't have seen on a New York street, and will find that he's bandaged the bleeding heel of Jesus. He'll learn to be dependent on people he'd have despised at home. He'll learn that if you rush and try to be first to Santiago, you'll get plantar fasciitis, and get there last. He won't need the Bible to tell him to "look at the birds of the air."[15] He will be, as the Baptist girl said, on the edges of things and will discover God's extraordinary preference for the periphery. Friendship will force him to ecumenism. Bigotry will be blistered and sweated out of him. He won't abandon his doctrine; he will understand it.

"After so much time walking the Road to Santiago," wrote Paulo Coelho, "the Road to Santiago began to walk me."[16] Well, fair enough, but in the law of the kingdom, each step is always and crucially our own.

It would be nice to be able to write about the Pilgrim Church, to illustrate the gradual approach of the church to the Holy City. But frankly, that's not what it looks like. We are told to believe that history is a linear business—that it starts at Creation, moves on through the Fall to redemption in Jesus, and then marches on to the final consummation. But has the church really moved forward at all? "Everything sacred is circular," said the native-American shaman Black Elk.[17] If the Christian view of history is right, he must be wrong. Or perhaps he's right, and the church isn't sacred at all.

The history of the church seems to be a series of depressingly repeating patterns. Every few hundred years the church suddenly rediscovers Jesus, and in a charismatic ecstasy of energy and holy passion starts to kindle the world. But then the gravelly voices of caution sound from high places in the church. They are generally male voices. "Our institutions are important. Tried and tested ways are best. Let's be realistic. Let's take the long view. Easy does it. We've seen all this before. It'll blow over." And the prophecies are self-fulfilling. It does blow over. The dreadlocks of the Jesus radicals go gray and fall out. The wild Christ-kids get elected to Congress, put on suits, and get flattered and promoted and busied into impotence. The Jesus dream is gone for another few generations. For those who live in the times of fire, it seems that a new world has dawned—that nothing will ever be the same again, that this is it. It seemed that way in Assisi, Wittenberg, and the Toronto Airport Church. But if we stand back, these are sparks in the overwhelming darkness.

I remember the first time I flew low over south Sudan at night. The sand and scrub were veiled in a thick, creamy black. Every few miles, though, there were points of light, all the more dazzling because of the surrounding dark. They were the camp-fires of the nomads. That's what Christian history is like. It's a dot-to-dot puzzle that links the fires of nomads, the people of the fringes, the crazy wanderers. And to my eye, they do seem to wander from water hole to water hole, rather than marching in any discernible line.

Phyllis Tickle has noted that every few centuries the church needs to hold a rummage sale to clear out the accumulated rubbish; the nonessentials; the clothes that seemed to be a good idea at the time but turned out to be ridiculous; the gadgets bought because of a salesman's silver tongue but which, far from being impossible to live without, proved pointless or dangerous.[18]

It's high time for another big clear-out. Let's build the pile high. There are two obvious things to chuck out. The first is the ugly, alien, proto-Germanic name "God." I've always found it far easier to have useful devotional feelings if I'm worshipping "the Holy One; Blessed be He," or "*El Shaddai*," or "*Elohim*." And fast behind "God" should come our name, "Christian." The Bible's not particularly keen on it, and the brand is fatally, irredeemably stained and compromised.[19] A recent survey in the United States asked respondents what they associated with the word *Christian*. "Anti-gay" was the most popular response, followed ignobly by "judgmental" and "hypocritical." "Christian" has to go. We've wrecked the word.

What should take its place? Well, although his notional followers have disgraced his movement, Jesus himself consistently commands respect. I'm cautious about suggesting a name that includes his for fear that when we foul up again, he'll get the blame; but perhaps the name will stop us messing up as badly as we've done until now.

I'm fond of "Jesus Freak." And that's not just because I'm in the throes of a midlife crisis (although I probably am) and it speaks of girls, guitars, joints, and beach parties. It seems to me to be theologically spot on. It tells of a people who leave the deadly, respectable things behind and, because they're obsessed with him, follow Jesus to the unrespectable edges. The weirdness of the name would force real discipleship. You wouldn't have people calling themselves Jesus Freaks because they thought it would increase their chances of being made partners in their law firms. The name would force the church to reclaim its historic constituency on the garbage tip.

But I can see that it won't catch on. So how about "Jesus Wanderer"? or "Jesus Follower"? I think God/the Holy One; Blessed be He, would approve. For there's no doubt that whether the margins in which you meet Jesus are metaphorical or physical, he, being God, is bound to be *moving*. He can't keep still. And he has an alarmingly clear preference for people who can't keep still.

3

BIAS TO THE WANDERER

Audubon kept a pinioned wild goose in confinement, and when the period of migration arrived, it became extremely restless, like all other migratory birds under similar circumstances; and at last it escaped. The poor creature then immediately began its long journey on foot.

—Charles Darwin[1]

Moses said to them, "Let no one leave any of [the manna] over until morning." But they did not listen to Moses; some left part of it until morning, and it bred worms and became foul.

—Exodus 16:19–20

If the blood flow through your heart reduces, you have pain. If it stops moving, you die. If water stops moving, it gets foul. This seems to illustrate a general rule. Time, the medium in which we swim, ticks inexorably on. It doesn't pause to take stock. "The heavens themselves run continually round," noted Robert Burton, "the sun riseth and setteth, the moon increaseth, stars and planets keep their constant motions, the air is still tossed by the winds, the waters ebb and flow, to their conservation no doubt, to teach us that we should ever be in motion."[2]

The first human beings like us that the Bible talks about were Cain and Abel. Their parents, Adam and Eve, didn't share our own history; they had distinctly unusual births.

Cain's and Abel's names were carefully chosen and ominous. *Cain* has a root that speaks of acquisition, possession, and real estate. We are meant to think of sharp suits, big cigars, share ownership, and huge grain silos. *Abel* means something like "the vanishing breath." We are meant to think of the mist that collects in the valley in the morning and is banished by the sun. Abel is the ephemeral one, the tramp, the hobo. In the story, he was a shepherd who would have followed his flocks wherever the grazing led, which was wherever the rain led. Although Cain was the firstborn, in a way we meet Abel before Cain. For Abel is like the man of the first of the two Creation stories in Genesis.[3] He exercises dominion over animals, and exists in harmony with the created order. Genesis 1:1–31 is a happy, upbeat story. It ends on an optimistic note: "God saw everything that he had made, and indeed, it was very good."[4] The harmony doesn't last long.

Cain's world is the world of Genesis 2: he was a tiller and keeper of the land.[5] It is in this second story that rebellion erupts, that the earth is wrenched brutally out of joint. The story has an unhappy legacy, and so did Cain. Cain's legacy was called civilization. It was a catastrophe. It came about like this:

Now the man knew his wife Eve, and she conceived and bore Cain, saying, "I have produced a man with the help of the LORD." Next she bore his brother Abel. Now Abel was a keeper of sheep, and Cain a tiller of the ground.

In the course of time Cain brought to the LORD an offering of the fruit of the ground, and Abel for his part brought of the firstlings of his flock, their fat portions. And the LORD had regard for Abel and his offering, but for Cain and his offering he had no regard. So Cain was very angry, and his countenance fell.

The LORD said to Cain, "Why are you angry, and why has your countenance fallen? If you do well, will you not be accepted? And if you do not do well, sin is lurking at the door; its desire is for you, but you must master it."

Cain said to his brother Abel, "Let us go out to the field." And when they were in the field, Cain rose up against his brother Abel, and killed him.

Then the LORD said to Cain, "Where is your brother Abel?" He said, "I do not know; am I my brother's keeper?" And the LORD said, "What have you done? Listen; your brother's blood is crying out to me from the ground! And now you are cursed from the ground, which has opened its mouth to receive your brother's blood from your hand. When you till the ground, it will no longer yield to you its strength; you will be a fugitive and a wanderer on the earth." Cain said to the LORD, "My punishment is greater than I can bear!

Today you have driven me away from the soil, and I shall be hidden from your face; I shall be a fugitive and a wanderer on the earth, and anyone who meets me may kill me." Then the LORD said to him, "Not so! Whoever kills Cain will suffer a sevenfold vengeance." And the LORD put a mark on Cain, so that no one who came upon him would kill him.

Then Cain went away from the presence of the LORD, and settled in the land of Nod, east of Eden. Cain knew his wife, and she conceived and bore Enoch; and he built a city, and named it Enoch after his son Enoch. To Enoch was born Irad; and Irad was the father of Mehujael, and Mehujael the father of Methushael, and Methushael the father of Lamech.

Lamech took two wives; the name of the one was Adah, and the name of the other Zillah. Adah bore Jabal; he was the ancestor of those who live in tents and have livestock. His brother's name was Jubal; he was the ancestor of all those who play the lyre and pipe. Zillah bore Tubal-cain, who made all kinds of bronze and iron tools.[6]

We are not told explicitly why God preferred Abel's sacrifice.[7] Is Yahweh showing us here the taste for blood that he inconsistently demonstrates throughout the Bible? Does Cain not give the first fruits—the cream of the crop—as we are told Abel does? Neither explanation really works. It looks like a simple, straightforward preference for Abel himself. And his lifestyle. Cain's response is fratricidal petulance. It is the attitude of sharkish, acquisitive businessmen the world over. Silence the competition. And that's what he does. But God does not smile on this early example of capitalist entrepreneurism. God's cross-examination catches Cain in a lie: "I don't know where my brother is." He was trying to be clever, in a smooth, urban, college-educated way. There was a sense in which he really didn't know where the essence, the "breath," of Abel had gone. We still don't. But, as Cain well knew, that wasn't what God was getting at. The fat farmer had added perjury to murder.

God moved straight to sentence. It was the sentence that Cain had been dreading. It struck at the very root of his existence. Indeed it cut his roots. It said that he had to sell his farm, trade in the harvester, give away the suits, and wander the earth. No more thrilling boardroom intrigue for him. He wouldn't have an address, let alone an expense account. He wouldn't be staying at the Sheraton; he'd be on the park bench outside, begging for a cup of tea. In other words, he had to become like his murdered brother.

In his panic, Cain really did think that his world had come to an end. The fall from magnate to hobo was so great that he heard God sentencing him to punishments that never fell from God's lips. "I shall be hidden from your face," he sobbed. But God never said anything of the kind. "Anyone who meets me may kill me," he went on, prompting an explicit reassurance from God that it would not happen.[8] Cain's whimpers were revealing. He didn't trust God, he was scared of men, and he was absolutely terrified of the natural world.

It has ever been so. Set a stockbroker loose in the Amazonian rain forest, and see what happens.

Then Cain stumbled away, his world in tatters. But only for a while. For the remarkable thing about the sentence is that it has never been served.

He went to the land of Nod, which literally means "the land of wandering." And what did he do there? Wander, as per the sentence? He did not. He went straight back to his old ways. He "*settled* in the land of Nod." Not only that, but in the very next verse he built a city called Enoch. It was named for his eldest son. The naming was not touching, but pathetic. It was yet another sign of Cain's insecurity and consequent conservatism. He was terrified of extinction, he wanted to write his name in the book of posterity, and he did it not by producing something new but by reiterating the old.

The city soon saw all the accoutrements of civilization: rising population (there is lots of breeding over the next few verses), culture (Jubal was "the ancestor of all those who play the lyre and pipe,"), and industry (Tubal-cain made "all kinds of bronze and iron tools," no doubt for trade). Soon Enoch was home to a loud, throbbing economy; and on its outskirts, shaggy and unkempt, looking in, their campfires flickering in the night, were the shepherds. They were the descendants of Jabal (for Abel was of course denied the chance to reproduce), and these wanderers

would have been cold-shouldered by their sophisticated rela-
tives, who recognized uncomfortably in them the features of the
shepherd whose blood stained their family record. As the city
expanded, its circumference increased. Its margins grew, and so
did the numbers on the margins: the edge people, the dispossessed. You don't herd sheep on the high street.

What had happened? Had God simply forgotten what he
said to Cain? Did God not see his rank disobedience?

He had not forgotten. He saw very clearly. C. S. Lewis said
that there is really only one law: everyone always gets what he
wants.[9] Cain wanted urban stability; he wanted not to wander.
And tragically, he got it. His punishment was to stay in the city, to
grow stagnant, to silt up, and to die. He could have had the stars,
the thyme on the mountainside, the cypress in the valley bottom,
the changing of the seasons, and the freedom of the wind. He
got the shopping mall, the pension policy, and the heart attack
that prevented him from drawing on the policy. Cain was frightened of Abel's name. He didn't like to think of himself as an
ephemeral, vaporous animal, soon gone. But living in the suburbs didn't change his ephemeral nature. He thought it would
make him safe. He lived smugly with the delusion of immortal-
ity. But he was mist, too, like his brother. If you are mist, it is best
to live as mist. It is foolish to pretend that you're a brick. You will
get more out of life by acknowledging what you are.

The sentence was being served. It would have been far
preferable to serve it in the circumstances originally envisaged

by God. But Cain decided that he would be disobedient. It was another fall, and another disaster. He thought he had escaped sentence. In fact he had made it worse. He became a wanderer, as the sentence specified, but not in a benign wilderness, which gave much more than it took. Instead he became psychologically rootless, an alien in a world that he had created himself, cut off from the intimate relationships with his fellows and with the created order for which he was designed. There is nowhere lonelier than a million-dollar condominium in a vast metropolis. The really crushing isolation is in a crowd. Some of my most tender moments of intimacy have been across a desert fire with people whose language I could not speak but whose tea and whose road I shared. Cain was a victim of the awful paradox: if you want real community, you need to be among the dispossessed, because dispossession generates vulnerability.

God's original sentence would have been redemptive. Cain missed the opportunity of redemption because he wrongly read it as punitive. That is often the way. The worst part of the sentence was one that God had not even pronounced. Cain pronounced it himself: "I shall be hidden from your face." It is an overstatement, but it carries with it a terrible truth. Throughout the Bible (with a crucial last-minute twist) God hates cities. He is much easier to find in the wilderness. He takes the side of the itinerant shepherd against the factory farmer.

Leon Kass postulates two alternative reasons for God's suspicion of tilling and all its connotations. The first is that the farmer becomes too masterful, too possessive, and too arrogant. He thinks he owns the land on which he is only a transient tenant. He arrogates to himself prerogatives that are really God's. The second is the converse of this. A farmer becomes a slave of the land and of the created order, looking dependently and polytheistically up to the sun and the rain.[10] I unhesitatingly plump for the first of these.[11] Kass doesn't allow himself the exegetical help of the New Testament. I think Jesus puts the reason beyond doubt. Building bigger barns isn't just stupid, dangerous, and dull, but blasphemous too.[12]

The cities grew and multiplied. Their presumption grew monstrous. God frustrated the building of the ultimate urban symbol, Babel. It wasn't just wanton petulance or vandalism. It was another attempt to be redemptive. For God tried again to turn the settlers into wanderers: "The LORD scattered them abroad from there over the face of all the earth, and they left off building the city."[13] But they don't leave off for long. It is not long before we see them again, hod in hand, scheme in head, buying their sheep from the nomads they were meant to be.

Abraham is too solid, too flawed, and too colorful to be a mere paradigm. Abram was seventy-five years old when he left Haran. Most seventy-five-year-olds are preparing for another sort of journey, and enjoying, while they can, the fruits of the wandering they have already done. One day I will write a book that imagines how the world would look if that old man had stayed in his tent cluster at Haran. It is bound to be an exciting book, because it will sketch a world dramatically different from our own. There would still have been sin and the need for redemption, but how would that redemption have come? There would have been wars, but the battle lines of the millennia would be in very different places. Perhaps if there had been no archetypal wanderer, there would have been no wandering. Perhaps human history would be the history of infighting between settlements.

But Abram did go. When I went to Haran, I admired Abram's obedience a little less. I could see why he would want to leave the place. It was hardly home for him anyway. He was of southern Mesopotamian stock, an Iraqi from near the now-devastated delta. He came from a family of gypsies. His father, Terah, seems to have been an aging hippie type who, for reasons hidden to the Bible, loaded up the family and headed a ridiculously long way north. It was unlikely to have been a search for grazing: you don't have to go that far to feed your goats. Perhaps Terah was a trader, selling beads or spices or pots.

When my bus pulled into Haran, the goat got off my lap and clattered off. The owner woke up, took his head off my shoulder, spat absent-mindedly onto my boot, and knelt with a handkerchief to wipe it off. There was blood in his spit. He kissed me. His breath was heavy with cannabis and beer.

I ate some small songbirds. The dark whirred. A dog urinated on my leg. I wondered vaguely if the rabies virus was carried in dog urine. A truck from Erzerum pulled in by the café. It was filled with deodorant bound for Damascus. The driver jumped down, came over, and sat at my table. He looked at me, offered me a cigarette, and lit one himself.

"You are English," he said, without a question mark.

"Yes," I said. "I'm sorry it shows."

"Don't be sorry about that or anything else." He pulled off his shoes and blew smoke into them. "But I am not English," he went on. "I am Turkish. And I am telling you to get out of this place. There is nothing here. Just dust and whores."

I hadn't seen any whores. Everyone seemed too tired for that sort of thing.

He stopped and lay back in his chair, watching me. I said nothing. He saw my notebook on the table. He pulled it over and started to read.

"You are here because of Abraham, I think?" he went on, after a while. "You think if you walk around here, some of his holiness will rub off on you? Let me tell you: he left here a very long time ago. You won't find him. But he was a good Muslim, peace be upon him."

There was a hot wind from Syria, smelling of dynamite and mice.

He waved his hand toward the night. "Out there," he said, "there is nothing. Just flies trying to eat rock. If you drive for three days, you will see a tree, and when you do, hide, because the Israelis will try to shoot you."

I tried to look interested and impressed.

"I suppose you're a bit like Abraham," I said, not believing it. "Same route. Same disturbance of family life."

"And same color," he added, fingering his mustache. "But no, let me tell you. That was a man, a proper man."

He was right.

Now the LORD said to Abram, "Go from your country and your kindred and your father's house to the land that I will show you. I will make of you a great nation, and I will bless you, and make your name great, so that you will be a blessing. I will bless those who bless you, and the one who curses you I will curse; and in you all the families of the earth shall be blessed." So Abram went.[14]

So Abram went. And so the rest of the Bible could continue.

Genesis is a very terse, tightly drafted book. But God seems uncharacteristically expansive in his command to Abram. Why couldn't he simply say, "Go to Canaan"? It is because he wants Abram's commitment to be complete. Abram could have gone to Canaan while still regarding himself as a Haranite and still a member of his family. But then the possession of Canaan would have been incomplete. Only if all the Mesopotamian and Turkish roots are dug up can Abram grow as deeply and intimately as he should into the land that God has prepared for him. The new rootedness is paradoxical. Abram will be rooted properly only if, and to the extent, that he remains a wanderer. Only someone who is committedly, incurably, rootlessly Bedouin can get the blessings ahead. It's the same with us. "If one just keeps on walking," wrote Søren Kierkegaard, "everything will be all right."[15] That's an overstatement, but as an approximation, it's not bad at all.

Take out a map of the Near East. Plot on it the journeying of the Patriarchs. It will look like a spider's web. And it seems that every few generations, after an episode of settlement, God uproots the Jews again. They don't like it much, but it has made them an incontestably great and brilliant people.

Abraham was a man. Wandering made him. And the nation of Israel was made in Sinai. It was there that the law was given. It was there that God showed himself, and his pastoral concern for his people, in ways that no other deity had ever done. They were the motley, bleating, disobedient sheep and goats; he was the desert shepherd. He wandered with them, beaten by the sun, setting up camp each night, lying on the same sand.

I once wrote a travel book that followed the route taken by the ark of the covenant. I wanted to call it *The Wanderings of God*.

"That'll never work," the marketing people told me. "Christians won't stomach the idea that God wanders. It suggests that he's vague."

Well, no it doesn't. It suggests that he sticks with his people, and that when they wander, he doesn't go off in a huff. God seems more himself during the Exodus than at any other time in the Old Testament. It's not that he is more forthcoming; he speaks loudly and passionately through the prophets later on. It's just that he seems more at home in a tent than a house. By nature he's a camper. Consistent with his earlier distaste for cities, he disapproves of artifice. Eat your lamb in the Bedouin way, he says, roasted over a fire. And no fancy sauces. Use the bitter herbs that you can pick in the wadi, and unleavened bread of the sort that the Sinai Arabs still bake over an upturned pot.[16] Keep it simple. I am a wild God: "You need make for me only an altar of earth . . . But if you make for me an altar of stone, do not build it of hewn stones; for if you use a chisel upon it you profane it."[17]

Moses himself was a proper Abel-ite. He never entered into possession of the promised land—perhaps it would have ruined him. And like that mist, he just vanished. He didn't even settle down postmortem. No elaborate sepulchre for him. "He was buried in a valley in the land of Moab, opposite Beth-peor, but no one knows his burial place to this day.[18]

Then came settlement. It seems that this was pragmatism on God's part. The Israelites had to have some place. But the intention was that they should be a pilgrim people with a post office box. Abraham's nomadism should be theirs. It was in the blood. God constantly reminded them of it. Yes, you have an address, but don't forget that you are gypsy stock: "When you have come into the land that the LORD your God is giving you as an inheritance to possess, and you possess it, and settle in it . . . you shall make this response before the LORD your God: 'A wandering Aramean was my ancestor.'"[19]

The same injunction is inherent in the great Jewish festivals. The Feast of Tabernacles requires the Jews to build shelters, to look up at the stars through the roof, and to say, "The sky is our real roof. We may live in Brooklyn, but that's not our real home." Passover reminds them of an urgent desert journey, with no time for proper packing. Each year at Passover the toast is, "Next year in Jerusalem." For them the journey is still incomplete. But here's the point: at a Jewish dinner table in a Jerusalem apartment overlooking the Western Wall, the toast is still the same—"Next year in Jerusalem." There is a sense in which arrival has never happened.

This is not just because of the precariousness of the Jews' hold on the land, bitterly and repeatedly demonstrated by the ebb and flow of Jews across the world: exile, return, exile, return, the destruction of the two temples and the nuclear threats of Iran. It is because, despite the physicality of the ancient promises to Abraham and his dependents, the genocidal successes of Joshua and the far-flung Jewish empire of Solomon, there's still a lot left to do—a lot of traveling to do.

"It's not just about geography, stupid," said Esti Herskowitz, an orthodox Jew from New York, over pizza in her house in a hilltop settlement just outside Jerusalem. "Don't be so shallow. It includes a whole host of desires: Messiah, redemption, the restoration of temple worship, the ingathering of exiles, and so on. Sure, we're in Jerusalem in a way, but there are lots of things on the list still to be ticked off."

So the Jews can't hang up their boots yet. Nor, I suspect, can they ever. In the Tibetan language, the word for human being is *a-Gro ba*. It means a "go-er"—someone who migrates. If a Tibetan stops migrating, he stops being a human being. Judaism has a similar idea. The expression "wandering Jew" is a tautology. If someone stops wandering, he stops being a Jew. Wandering is a formula for supreme blessing, because the Blesser himself is a wanderer.

Nonetheless, God left his tent or allowed it to be carried indoors to the holy dark in the temple. There, between the cherubim on the ark of the covenant, God sat, fed with the blood from the gigantic abattoir that the temple was. He blessed the builder. But in the story of the building of the temple, there is a tone of reluctance. The temple is something David and Solomon want more than God does. God graciously goes along with it, because they are honestly trying to honor him. But it is easier to hear the authentic Sinai intonation of Yahweh in the anti-temple prophets. And there were plenty of them. Authentic religion, they said, is by definition a religion of the trail. Be like the Rechabites, said God, through the stern Jeremiah. They resolutely kept to the old ways, refusing to build a house, sow seed, plant, or even own a vineyard. Their ancestor had told them, "You shall live in tents all your days, that you may live many days in the land where you reside."[20] That's what they did, and they were rewarded.[21] Bruce Chatwin summarizes well:

> [God] appears in the Burning Bush and in the Pillar of Fire. He is everything that Egypt is *not.* Yet he will allow himself the doubtful honour of a Temple—and regret it: "They have set their abomination in the house which is called by my name, to pollute it." (Jeremiah 7:30) . . . The prophets Isaiah, Jeremiah, Amos and Hosea were nomadic revivalists who howled abuse at the decadence of civilisation. By sinking roots in the land, by 'laying house to house and field to field,' by turning the Temple into a sculpture gallery, the people had turned from their God. *How long, O Lord, how long?* . . . 'Until the cities be wasted' . . . The prophets looked to a Day of Restoration when the Jews would return to the frugal asceticism of nomadic life. In the vision of Isaiah they are promised a Saviour, whose name would be Emmanuel, and who would be a herdsman."[22]

God seems to like nomads because they are like him. Their values are his. They are clean, and they value relationship.

Throughout the ancient world, wanderers are good, and the sluggish stay-at-homes are not. It's impossible to point to an epic hero who's a couch potato. In the epic world, he who goes, wins. The Greeks trounce the Trojans, who just sit behind their walls. The Odyssey *finishes* when Odysseus finds his way home to Penelope. A modern writer might well want to say that the really interesting part of the story was how they patched up their marriage after Odysseus' long Cyclops-blinding, witch-entrancing absence, but that's not how Homer saw it.

It is not just that the wanderers are more interesting. Homer and Hesiod knew very well that there was a difference between being exciting and being morally good. But they repeatedly portray the nomads as upright law-keepers.

That's my experience too. I have only ever been beaten up, robbed, and threatened in cities. The bigger the city, the bigger the thrashing, and the sharper the knife. I have spent a fair amount of my life traipsing across wilderness, entrusting my life, my goods, and my sanity to nomadic strangers. We can argue about my sanity, but they have guarded my life and my goods as their own. Even migratory animals are less aggressive than stay-at-home species. It makes evolutionary sense. If you have a long way to go, your energy is better spent trudging than on testosterone-fueled feuding.

The bonds between nomads are necessarily closer than those between urban men. It's a matter of survival. Laurens Van der Post tells of Kalahari bushmen, who know that a hunting party fifty miles away has killed, that it has killed a kudu, and the exact time of its arrival back at camp. When the bushmen learned of the white man's telegraph, they presumed that it worked by telepathy, as their own communications did.[23] Just imagine the intimacy of relationship that sort of mental intertwining creates. Those nomads (before they were destroyed by us) had a degree of community that we poor, shallow, lonely urbanites can only imagine.

Nomad hospitality is, of course, legendary, and an important survival mechanism. Protection of the visitor is a sacred duty. When God comes to visit, Abraham does what any Bedouin would do:

> The LORD appeared to Abraham by the oaks of Mamre, as he sat at the entrance of his tent in the heat of the day. He looked up and saw three men standing near him. When he saw them, he ran from the tent entrance to meet them, and bowed down to the ground. He said, "My lord, if I find favor with you, do not pass by your servant. Let a little water be brought, and wash your feet, and rest yourselves under the tree. Let me bring a little bread, that you may refresh yourselves, and after that you may pass on" . . . Abraham hastened into the tent to Sarah, and said, "Make ready quickly three measures of choice flour, knead it, and make cakes. Abraham ran to the herd, and took a calf, tender and good, and gave it to the servant, who hastened to prepare it.

Then he took curds and milk and the calf that he had prepared, and set it before them; and he stood by them under
the tree while they ate.[24]

I have been treated like God countless times. The Genesis
account is a perfect contemporary description of the scene: the
gentle but absolute insistence; the motion to be seated; the rak-
ing of the fire; the pouring of tea and the making of bread; the
murmured orders to a little silent woman who won't catch your
eye; the sound of an animal being dragged through the sand,
and its last gurgle. The hosts can never afford this hospitality.
The animal is a big thing for them. But they know, somehow,
that it will not only be all right if they give it, but bad if they
don't.

It is easy to romanticize Bedouin hospitality. Travelers'
blogs are full of breathless accounts of "gen-u-ine desert grace,"
when the reality is that the German or Milwaukeean tour group
has paid a huge premium for the privilege of a cup of tea and a
seat on a flea-ridden carpet, all of which goes to buy Marlboro
Lights and the new Toyota Land Cruiser. And of course the
whole system of hospitality is based on self-interest. It's a form
of reciprocal altruism, as the zoologists would say. You scratch
my back, and I'll scratch yours. If you don't feed Ahmed today,
he'll let you die next week when you're out of water and four
days from the next well.

But for all the cynicism, good behavior is its own reward.

Doing the right thing, even out of duty, changes souls. Nomads smile more. Because they have nothing, they have everything, and so they have more to smile about.

When men stop wandering, it all goes wrong. That is what the story of Sodom is about.[25]

Sodom was a town. Many in it had abandoned the desert ways. Two travelers arrived. (They happened to be angels.) Lot greeted them in the traditional way, insisting they stay with him and giving them the usual feast. But the house was surrounded by townies—aggressive, bored, listless men with dead eyes. We've all seen them at street corners. There was nothing to do in Sodom if you had lost the art of conversation you learn in a tent and didn't like looking at the stars. So they proposed a gang rape.

Lot was outraged: "I beg you, my brothers, do not act so wickedly. Look, I have two daughters who have not known a man; let me bring them out to you, and do to them as you please; only do nothing to these men, for they have come under the shelter of my roof."[26]

It is a shocking passage. It illustrates the crucial importance of nomadic hospitality. It is better to let your virgin daughters be gang-raped than to breach the ancient canons. The Sodom story has nothing specifically to do with homosexuality, of course. Lot's outrage would have been just as great if the gang had tried a knifepoint robbery.

Sodom, famously, paid a terrible price for its failure to remember the edicts governing wandering life. The story is an indication that God expects urbanites to behave as morally as noble tramps. Lot was saved because he remained at heart a Bedouin. Today he'd have a Volkswagen camper van and wear beads that he'd brought back from Kathmandu. His wife looked back wistfully at the dubious joys of settlement and was turned into a pillar of salt. We've seen it before in the Cain and Abel story. The penalty for wanting to be a settler is that you become one. Pillars of salt don't go on exhilarating marches from well to well.

So traveling helps you to be good, to feel good, and to be alive. "There is no happiness for him who does not travel, Rohita!" observes the Aitareya Brahmana, an early comment on Hindu Vedic ritual. "Thus have we heard. Living in the society of men, the best man becomes a sinner . . . therefore, wander!"[27] That great mystic Thoreau, of whom Christians are so suspicious, similarly saw movement as inextricably connected to the business of being human: "We do not commonly live our life out in full; we do not fill all our pores with our blood; we do not inspire and expire fully and entirely enough . . . We live but a fraction of our life. Why do we not let in the flood, raise the gates, and set all our wheels in motion?"[28]

It's because we are bound to places and possessions, and befouled with all the moral detritus that comes with them, says the Bible. We are Cains, so terrified of wildness and aliveness that we bulldoze it whenever we see it, whether that means killing our wandering brother, penning nomads in compounds, or hanging gypsies.

There is another strand too. One of the things that many others have commented on is the childlikeness of the wanderers. Yes, they smile, but it is not the knowing smile of the big grown-up lawyer. It is the trusting smile of a playful child. There's a hilarity about the Bedouin camp that you never otherwise see outside the nursery.

One night during a long traverse of central Sinai, we had had our bread and our tuna (yes, some desert customs have gone, but cans of tuna don't seem to produce moral debility). We made a newspaper into a ball and kicked it around the sand. I slipped and fell. My kind, loyal Bedouin guides fell down, too, paralytic with laughter. They were speechless for a good ten minutes. The event was reenacted, with the laughter recapitulated, for the next fortnight. I next saw that response in my four-year-old son, Tom. Most adults (and all accountants), would have smiled solicitously, brushed me off, and gone back to their books.

This childlikeness isn't feeble-mindedness. Neither is it a mere absence of anything else to laugh at. If I had fallen over in the company of the same people when they were watching *The Simpsons* on Egyptian TV in a Nuweiba house, the response would have been the same. I have noticed the same thing among restless Europeans. The best-traveled people, the ones who have seen the most, are the ones who remain the most capable of seeing the world through the eyes of children. Children's eyes don't have the spiritual cataracts that blur the vision of the worldly-wise. They see color, mystery, and excitement where we see only a parking lot. They are immeasurably richer than we are.

Those cataracts seem to be caused by a sedentary life. Children don't get them, because everything is new. If you're traveling, every glimpse is new too.

If your world is gray, and you see the same slice of the world through your office window every day, it is not surprising if you become morbidly attached to your little slice and consumed with the desire to assert your title to it. It is not surprising that you become unhappy, cynical, jaded, and fat. Get up, get out. "The great affair is to move," said Robert Louis Stevenson, and he was right.[29]

There was another great traveler who stood squarely in the tradition of Abel and Lot. He described himself as a shepherd, as opposed to a tiller. His birth was announced in terms of the holy anarchy of the road, terrifying to Wall Street, but which describes the joyful experience of all nomads: "He has filled the hungry with good things, and sent the rich away sent empty."[30] I'm on the edge of things, he said, and I'm here for the people on the edge. He said that only the eyes of children could see what his real kingdom was about. His name, of course, was Jesus.

4

THE GOD WHO WALKS

There is always some madness in love,
but there is always some reason in madness.

—Friedrich Nietzsche[1]

The Gospels smell of the road as *The Odyssey* smells
of the sea.

A devoutly atheistic friend picked up the Bible on my desk.
He flicked through it and threw it contemptuously down.

"The most interesting stuff in there is the maps," he said.
God more or less agrees.

You hit the road as soon as you open the New Testament.
The genealogy in Matthew clunks along with the rhythm of
footsteps. Time is even divided up in the summary by reference to journeys or great nomads: "So all the generations from
Abraham to David are fourteen generations; and from David to
the deportation to Babylon, fourteen generations; and from the
deportation to Babylon to the Messiah, fourteen generations."[2]

The first recorded response to Jesus of anyone outside his

family is to leap on a camel and make an immensely long and dangerous journey across the Middle and Near East: "Wise men from the East came to Jerusalem, asking, 'Where is the child?'"[3] The star travels too: "There, ahead of them, went the star . . . until it stopped over the place where the child was."[4] If Christianity is accurately described as a movement (and it certainly is), it was preceded by a literal movement.

To me there is, in the period between the testaments, a sense of paralysis. It is as if a growing flower has been frozen. The tension builds; it is all the greater for being a static tension. Nothing moves. And then Jesus explodes into the world, and suddenly there is movement everywhere. The ice around the flower melts, water flows, the flower bursts out with the sort of growth you see when the cameras are speeded up. Aslan is on the move, and everything with him.

The wise men were the first Christian pilgrims. They were probably Zoroastrian astrologers, who'd never be invited to speak in a mainstream evangelical church. They set the pattern for all subsequent pilgrimages: they came, they arrived, and they went back home.[5]

As soon as they left, another journey breathlessly began. "Get up," said an angel. It is a fairly typical angelic command. You will search the Bible in vain for an angel telling anyone to sit down, relax, and catch up with the celebrity gossip. "Get up, take the child and his mother, and flee to Egypt."[6]

Whichever route they took, I have taken the same road. I

expect they went due south, along the rolling road through the Judean hills. Stones stick out of the ground like bones. In the spring there is a green fog of grass. By July all color is sucked out of the land. There are old, writhing olives; little vineyards; and small, brave clusters of white, flat-roofed houses. On the hilltops, like stranded battleships, are the settlements, bristling with armor and antennae, watching.

They would have passed through checkpoints manned by bored Roman conscripts who would rather be in Naples. Today the checkpoints are manned by bored Israeli conscripts who would rather be at Harvard. At Hebron, the Holy Family would have passed the tombs of those other great travelers, the Patriarchs, who had paced these roads many hundreds of years before. Joseph and Mary were pious and very orthodox Jews. It would have been strange, on the run though they were, if they had not sought the blessing from the shadowy afterlife of those hard old paradigmatic nomads who, in the paradoxical providence of God, had formed a nation by continuing to walk. A new sort of nation was in the making. And it depended, too, on a man and his wife continuing to walk.

So they did. If they didn't go directly south, perhaps they turned east from Hebron, winding down through the ravines to the Dead Sea, looking over through the haze to Moab and Arabia. If they did, they then turned south along the Wadi Arabah—the extension into the Near East of the Great Rift Valley that divides the earth all the way down into east Africa, and up which the very first Palestinians had come. They would have heard for the first time the fluting of the wind through the African whistling thorn, been mocked by the Tristram's Grackles that now eat tourists' sandwiches in the lay-bys, seen how the sun flattens the land at noon and then slashes it with shadow, and tasted the Red Sea before they saw it. Then they would have turned up the ancient road across Sinai—the road that later became the Hajj road, carrying travelers from north Africa to Mecca, and along which T. E. Lawrence rode impossibly fast from Aqaba to get gold from Suez to pay off his looting tribesman. I hate the road. It makes me feel as desolate as it is. Even the flies are bored.

But almost certainly they went the other way, turning west at Hebron, meandering through citrus groves,[7] and hitting the sea somewhere near Rafah, at the south end of the Gaza Strip. Then it smelled of herrings and resin: now it smells of tear gas, antiseptic, and sewage.

The coast road was one of the main arteries of the Near East. Joseph and Mary would have jumped with their baby out of the way of careering chariots that filled their eyes with grit. They would have been pressed, probably pointlessly, for *baksheesh* at the checkpoints. To their right were the flat, white beaches where nobody goes, the murmur of the sea, and gulls from Crete. The road is very flat, and either very hot or very cold. They would have slept out on a blanket in the places where the camel trains stopped. Little, urgent camel ticks would have scuttled over them as soon as they lay down. In the morning they would have pulled them, big as olives, out of their groins and off their backs. They would not have realized when they crossed into Egypt.

Eventually Herod the baby-killer died, and the family returned to Palestine. And there Joseph "made his home in a town called Nazareth."[8] "Provincial" just doesn't begin to describe it. This was nowhere. When Nathanael asked, "Can anything good come out of Nazareth?"[9] it was a perfectly reasonable question. God was using the methods he had always used. He works always at the edges, where the dogs prowl, using the most improbable material. He has never, ever sought to start the ripple of any significant wave at the center of society, or use the most objectively promising human material. Any headhunter would be appalled at his recruitment criteria.

God let the boy grow up normally. He didn't send him to some top-ranking private school, still less to a high-powered theological seminary. Jesus learned to make chairs, sweep up sawdust, and say the Shabbat prayers. It really was very careless of God. That carelessness is called incarnation.

The time came for Jesus' public ministry to start. It was announced by the sort of character we should now come to expect: a ragged, dreadlocked desert-dweller called John, who lived (guess where?) well outside even the most dubiously respectable suburb. Logistically, he had no idea at all how to plan a mission. People were going to have to walk miles through a desert to get there, and how many people would do that? When, against all odds, he got some really influential society figures coming, instead of smooching them and showing them to the seats in the front row, he abused them violently and personally, choosing to point out that their morality meant they couldn't with a straight face claim descent from the great wanderer. "Bear fruit worthy of repentance. Do not presume to say to yourselves, 'We have Abraham as our ancestor.'"[10] He had a taste in dress that would make church ushers say, "Excuse me, sir, but . . ." and a diet that would faze the stoutest and most enterprising hostess.[11] When he started shrieking about Jesus, he used the language of travel: "Prepare the *way* of the Lord; make his paths straight."[12]

By the standards of the suburbs and the center, it was really not a great warm-up act. But people came: "The people of Jerusalem and all Judea were going out to him, and all the region along the Jordan."[13] Jesus generated pilgrimage at his birth. He was generating it again. The theme would be repeated again and again.

Jesus went from the Galilee to the Jordan to be baptized by John,[14] and then he was immediately off into the wilderness, where he was tempted.[15] The traditional site of the temptation, which has no historical corroboration whatever, is near the Monastery of the Temptation, overlooking Jericho. The site is tremendously unimportant. If the temptation was not there, it was somewhere like it. Jesus might have walked for hundreds of miles in those forty days, each mile looking like the one before it. Hot rocks that taunt you with their antiquity and, therefore, your irrelevance. Skull stones with empty eyes that remind you that you are food for worms. Little birds that will go home to a mate when you won't. Big, soaring birds that you resent because they can see the lights of Jerusalem, and you can't. Little scurrying things that you grow to loathe because they live here and don't join you in protesting about it. But worst, the interrogating silence, the terrible silence that probes into the emptiness that you used to call yourself. The silence that shouts mocking things into the emptiness that is you so that you can't miss the accusing echo that says, "You thought you were a man of substance: Listen. There's nothing there." It was landscape like this that broke my heart and nearly my mind during a long, emetic time in Sinai. Only an extraordinary tenderness put it back together.

Jesus' temptation was a rerun of the Exodus, although this time there was no disobedience. Although no moral cleansing was necessary, the experience was evidently necessary for some reason, just as the Exodus had been. In the desert, Israel faced its demons, comfort and food: "Let's go back to Egypt. Let's be salaried wage slaves with an assurance of food on the table rather than free men with all the vicissitudes of nomadism. We're fantasizing about steak. This desert food is dreadful." The Israelites covered themselves in shame. In the desert, Jesus faced the same temptations and much, much more. He came out in glory.

Then he started preaching, but in Galilee, for goodness' sake.[16] It's like saying that the whole thrust of your campaign for the evangelization of the United States will be in Hawaii.

Yes, there will be occasional appearances in New York, but the key speeches will be in a school hall in Honolulu. It's the completely consistent topsy-turvy strategy of the topsy-turvy kingdom. Jesus thought people would travel. He was right. And once they got to him, they just kept traveling, because that's what he did. It was the original road show.

From the start, the Jesus road show was a sociable business. He wanted people to walk with. He met them when he was walking: "As he walked by the Sea of Galilee, he saw two brothers."[17] He called them along for a walk ("Follow me"), not for a lecture in doctrine. If his followers could have seen then where it would lead (to death by spearing—Matthew and Thomas; to being crucified upside down—Peter; to being stoned to death—Matthias; to being flayed alive and crucified—Bartholomew; and so on), perhaps they would never have come. The road is often merciful, hiding the hard places from us at times when we are weak. All that we are required to do is to put one foot in front of the other. And then do it again.

Jesus extended the invitation to come on pilgrimage. Simon Peter, Andrew, James, and John "immediately" accepted and went. The Holy Spirit is a very careful choreographer: he even put Zebedee, the father of James and John, in the picture so the parallel with the faithfulness of Abraham was complete. Not only did they all leave their livelihoods, their houses, and their own schemes, but they left their kindred too: "Immediately [James and John] left the boat *and their father*, and followed him."[18]

With his band of confused, fascinated men and women, Jesus *wandered* through the least strategically located part of Palestine, proclaiming and demonstrating the kingdom: "Jesus went throughout Galilee, teaching in their synagogues and proclaiming the good news of the kingdom and curing every disease and every sickness among the people."[19] His pilgrimage caused more pilgrimage. The pilgrims weren't all curious tourists, although they were all curious. They wanted *results*: "So his fame spread throughout all Syria, and they brought to him all the sick, those who were afflicted with various diseases and pains, demoniacs, epileptics, and paralytics, and he cured them. And great crowds followed him from Galilee, the Decapolis, Jerusalem, Judea, and from beyond the Jordan."[20]

That's another theme: pilgrimages *do* things. The travels of Abraham inked in the covenant and laid the foundations of a nation; the Exodus transformed a people and won a land; the Baptist girl at my dinner got a husband, was healed of hay fever, and became a Jesus Freak.

Then came the Sermon on the Mount, which is all about the people on the edges—the sort of people you meet, eat with, walk with, bed down, and *become* if you walk from town to town, but would never see if you drive along the freeway in your air-conditioned limo.

By and large the Sermon on the Mount is utterly irrelevant to most modern churches. It might as well not be there. Our lives, our businesses, and our mission strategies are constructed very specifically according to precisely the principles so clearly denounced by Jesus. If we had been running his campaign, we'd have thrown money not at lepers, but at management consultants and lobbyists, who would be able to put in a shrewd word in the Pharisaic and even (if you got a really good guy on the case) the Roman hierarchy. And Jesus certainly wouldn't have been allowed to walk. It's dangerous, time-consuming, and sends out all the wrong signals. A nice chariot, perhaps, with the logo on the side. Or a well-brushed horse of impeccable breeding.

Someone on his feet all day knows that his feet and his belly matter. Gnosticism doesn't survive the twentieth mile. "Your kingdom come. Your will be done, on *earth* [on the trail, on the outskirts of the towns] as it is in heaven. Give us this day our daily bread."[21] The plea for daily bread is a prayer to be sustained in that outpost of the kingdom for which you have prayed and in which you walk, bleed, and make love.

One of the constant refrains in pilgrim tales is that you find food when you need it; that you meet at the crossroads the person who knows the way; that when you fall, the backpack of the next stranger has in it a dressing that exactly covers your wound. These observations are usually made with surprise and wonder. Perhaps this is the general rule, but we are so smothered with superfluity we don't notice that our needs are met by solutions intimately tailored to them. We worry about our needs being met because we have never noticed they are. What is certainly true is that when we prise ourselves away, be it ever so slightly, from the mind-bogglingly complex raft of support mechanisms we wrongly call our lives and that we think we need, we are immediately shocked and delighted at the apparent beneficence of the world. It seems to have been set up for us. By the end of the second day on the road, the wonder has started to breed trust.

I panted to the top of a rise somewhere near Annapurna Base Camp and stopped to pull off the leeches. I had taken off my shirt and was trying to burn one out of my armpit with a cigarette lighter without setting fire to my underarm hair when a voice said, "Will you allow me?" It was a Buddhist monk, originally from Chicago, called, unmystically, Sam. He had been rolling joints from the cannabis bushes that grow along the path. He took one out of a satchel, which was all that he carried, lit it, touched the leech with the hot tip, picked it off and put it gently on the path. He offered me a drink from his water bottle. I drank, and then he told me that he had syphilis. He saw me looking worried, and he laughed.

"You don't get it from water bottles, man. You get it from bad girls in Saigon. But it's all under control now, thanks to Jesus."

"Thanks to *Jesus*?"

"Yep. He knew precisely the right antibiotic for it. It was the only antibiotic they had, in the only shop there was, in the only village there was for a hundred miles in the north of Thailand, where I was when it hit me. If he hadn't been merciful, and if he hadn't known his pharmacology, it would have rampaged through me, I wouldn't have survived to become happily celibate, and I would never have started out on the Lotus Path."

Three thousand miles away I could hear evangelical toes curling.

"But why give thanks to Jesus when you're plainly a Buddhist?"

"Why, he's a Buddha, my friend. And don't you know what he said?" And as he sat there, leaning against the great green wall of the Himalaya that leapt all the way up to Tibet, and as the brown melt water from the glacier chased toward India, and as the leech squeezed through his bootlace hole, he recited, word perfect, one of the most famous passages from the Gospel of Matthew: "I tell you, do not worry about your life, what you will eat or what you will drink, or about your body, what you will wear. Is not life more than food, and the body more than clothing? Look at the birds of the air [and he pointed to the lammergeier hanging in the wind]; they neither sow nor reap nor gather into barns, and yet your heavenly Father feeds them."[22]

There are neater sermon illustrations than Sam, it's true.

All of the Sermon on the Mount is best read when you're walking. "Do not worry about tomorrow, for tomorrow will bring worries of its own."[23] That's easier to believe when you are living as intensely in the present as pain, joy, and a new landscape with every blink force you to do. "Everyone who searches, finds."[24] Everyone who takes to the road is searching, and no one comes back saying, "That was a waste of time." There is a 100 percent *encounter* rate. But in the world at large, and in the Christian world in particular, very few people seem to have found what Jesus is talking about in the Sermon on the Mount. That means, if Jesus is telling the truth, that very few people are searching in the way he meant. That, after all, is precisely what he said a few lines later, wielding yet again the imagery of travel: "Enter through the narrow gate; for the gate is wide and the road is easy that leads to destruction, and there are many who take it. For the gate is narrow and the road is hard that leads to life, and there are few who find it."[25] I suppose he's right about that.

A couple of chapters later, Jesus called Matthew. The gospel uses a formula that is now familiar, but this time there is a twist pertinent to our tale:

"As Jesus was walking along, he saw a man called Matthew sitting at the tax booth; and he said to him, 'Follow me.' And he got up and followed him."[26] So Jesus was walking. Matthew was sitting. Walking is better than sitting—better for your soul and your eternal destiny, as well as your back and your mood. In order to follow Jesus, you have to stop sitting and start walking. That's what Matthew did, and so the wanderers multiply and the wandering goes on: "Jesus went on from there,"[27] "Jesus went about all the cities and villages,"[28] and so on.

And then, having been given an apprenticeship in the ways

of the road, it is time for the followers to do some pilgrimage by themselves. They never leave the jurisdiction of Jesus: they are on his road, and so never walk out of the kingdom. They don't stop being disciples. They are still following him, but he will not always be physically there. They need to learn to beg, to trust, to travel light, to move constantly on and on, and importantly, to see as an index of spiritual worth the extent to which their hosts adopt those old-fashioned nomadic values of hospitality. If they treat you as a Bedouin would, says Jesus, they're kosher. If they treat you as an urbanite who has lost touch with those central values, they're not. There is a specific reference to the hospitality-breaching sin of Sodom, just in case anyone misses the point:

> These twelve [disciples] Jesus sent out with the following instructions: "Go nowhere among the Gentiles, and enter no town of the Samaritans, but go rather to the lost sheep of the house of Israel. As you go, proclaim the good news, "The kingdom of heaven has come near." Cure the sick, raise the dead, cleanse the lepers, cast out demons. You received without payment; give without payment. Take no gold, or silver, or copper in your belts, no bag for your journey, or two tunics, or sandals, or a staff; for laborers deserve their food. Whatever town or village you enter, find out who in it is worthy, and stay there until you leave. As you enter the house, greet it. If the house is worthy, let your peace come upon it; but if it is not worthy, let your peace return to you. If anyone

will not welcome you or listen to your words, shake off the dust from your feet as you leave that house or town. Truly I tell you, it will be more tolerable for the land of Sodom and Gomorrah on the day of judgment than for that town.[29]

Matthew is an economical book. These traveling instructions are very detailed, and therefore presumably very important. The way and the spirit of traveling seem to be inextricably bound up with the objective. It is shocking to note, yet again, how little doctrine they are taught to teach. The sermon they are told to preach is exactly seven words long in English; it is six in Greek. The journey, the manner of the journey, and the dramatic demonstrations of it (healings, raisings from the dead, exorcisms) form far and away the greater part of the sermon. When John asks Jesus, "Are you the one who is to come, or are we to wait for another?"[30] Jesus doesn't give a theological exposition of the historic Messianic expectations. He simply says: tell him what has happened along the road among the pilgrims and the people on the dung heap through which we walked.[31]

Between life-changing sermons, Jesus was *of course* walking. And walking. "He left that place";[32] "He departed";[33] "Jesus left that place and went away to the district of Tyre and Sidon"[34] (quite a journey, and an interesting one throughout history; I've lain awake at night in Sidon, listening to popping mortar shells, and didn't like it much); "After Jesus had left [the district of Tyre and Sidon], he passed along the Sea of Galilee, and he went up the mountain";[35] "Jesus came into the district of Caesarea Philippi";[36] "he left Galilee and went to the region of Judea beyond the Jordan"[37] (looking back, probably, over the orange groves of Jericho, along the route that Joshua's conquering army took, through a plain of cracked earth and dog bones, to the place where he struggled alone with Satan); "Jesus was going up to Jerusalem"[38] (the final climax builds); "they were leaving Jericho"[39] (it is harder to get in these days—the logistics of traveling in the Palestinian territories are nightmarish and unpredictable); "they had . . . reached Bethphage, at the Mount of Olives"[40] (where there is a very fine hummus shop); "he entered Jerusalem."[41]

He then walked to his own death, carrying a burden heavier than anyone has ever carried, and having said ominously to his followers that unless they continued to follow him even there, they were not worthy of him. Lose your life on the road with me, and you will find it: keep it in the combination safe at home or in the office, and you'll be robbed for sure.[42] Following isn't all about happy healings and spring flowers in Galilee, but the only real security is in the joyful insecurity of the nomad.

You can take a similar tour in the footsteps of Jesus through Mark and John. Mark follows the route-tracing finger of Matthew very closely. John is particularly keen to emphasize Jesus' involvement in the formal Jewish pilgrimages of Passover[43] and Sukkot.[44]

In Luke, Jesus' peregrinations begin while he is still a fetus.

The pregnant Mary "set out and went with haste to a Judean town in the hill country, where she . . . greeted Elizabeth."[45] Bruce Chatwin notes that babies rocked at the rhythm of natural walking calm down and stop crying, citing it as evidence that humans are designed as walking mammals and that we are happy only if we behave in the way we're designed.[46] If that is right, Jesus was introduced very early to that crucial element of incarnation. As soon as he had sense receptors capable of detecting walking sway, he felt it: his mother was a great walker.

The birth narrative in Luke is a hurried succession of journeys. The family went from Nazareth to Bethlehem because of the census, and there Jesus was born.[47] Shepherds came to see the newborn child.[48] Today, when they can get through, Mercedes tour buses disgorge overheated tourists in Manger Square. Sweating and credulous, they squeeze into the underground chamber and weepily, creakingly bow to kiss the star that marks the place where Jesus, or Adonis, or very possibly no one at all, was born.[49]

The shepherds, like so many other Jesus-followers (remember those newly invited disciples, who left "immediately"), think there is urgency: "They went with haste" to Bethlehem.[50] Their motives are unclear: "Let us go now to Bethlehem and see this thing that has taken place."[51]

They probably weren't very introspective men, and probably their motives were as mixed as human motives usually are. Perhaps they wanted to convince themselves that the angelic apparitions weren't pathological; perhaps they were aching for the Savior the angel had promised. But it sounds more like that characteristic fascination with Jesus: that magnetism that still pulls people from Atlanta to Rome and Sydney to Nazareth. It is not surprising that it pulled them over the steep, stony, ankle-breaking fields to the shed where God was screaming and vomiting. After they had seen, they went. They didn't just drift away. We're specifically told that they "returned, glorifying and praising God for all they had heard and seen."[52] Invitation, start, journey, arrival, return. The pattern recurs.

On the eighth day Jesus, as a good Jewish boy should be, was taken up to the Jerusalem temple—one of those mini pilgrimages designed to keep Jewish feet itchy and fit—and then the family headed up on the old road through the hills of Samaria (one of the loveliest and most inflammable routes in Israel, marked by command towers and suspicion. The last time I was there, we stopped to eat hot dogs at an Israeli Army canteen. "Every week the Army here catches a young boy who wants to blow himself up on a bus in Israel," said my minder. "Every week. You don't hear it on the news. It's not news. It's normal").

The next time we hear of Jesus in Luke, he is yet again on pilgrimage. His devout parents have taken him to Jerusalem for Passover.[53] Soon begins the tour that we have followed in Matthew. The message is the same: "Jesus was asked by the Pharisees when the kingdom of God was coming, and he answered, 'The kingdom of God is not coming with things that can be observed; nor will they say, "Look, here it is!" or "There it is!" For, in fact, the kingdom of God is among you."[54]

Get up, get out, wake up, walk on, open your eyes, ask for new eyes: you'll see it if you are really looking for it. It's here, it's now, it's on the road that I'm walking, and it's here because *I'm* walking. Do you want to see it? Walk that road too. You're blinded by indolence, by living in the center. It's all happening at the edges, in the forgotten places, in the places you can't get to by car or where your auto insurers wouldn't let you drive, among the people you've put out with the trash. Reclaim the ability to be taken by surprise, and you'll see it there, glistening so brightly you will never believe you could have missed it.

He walked and walked and walked, and then he was nailed to a piece of wood on a garbage heap outside a city and stopped walking for a while. His heart stopped; his breath stopped. He was dead, and because it was hot, he started to decompose.

Three days later a very odd thing happened. Two of his disciples were going to a village called Emmaus, about seven miles from Jerusalem. They were talking about some curious rumors they had heard in relation to Jesus' grave.

While they were talking and discussing, Jesus himself came near and went with them, but their eyes were kept from recognizing him. And he said to them, "What are you discussing with each other while you walk along?" They stood still, looking sad. Then one of them, whose name was Cleopas, answered him, "Are you the only stranger in Jerusalem who does not know the things that have taken place there in these days?" He asked them, "What things?" They replied, "The things about Jesus of Nazareth, who was a prophet mighty in deed and word before God and all the people, and how our chief priests and leaders handed him over to be condemned to death and crucified him. But we had hoped that he was the one to redeem Israel. Yes, and besides all this, it is now the third day since these things took place. Moreover, some women of our group astounded us. They were at the tomb early this morning, and when they did not find his body there, they came back and told us that they had indeed seen a vision of angels who said that he was alive. Some of those who were with us went to the tomb and found it just as the women had said; but they did not see him." Then he said to them, "Oh, how foolish you are, and how slow of heart to believe all that the prophets have declared! Was it not necessary that the Messiah should suffer these things and then enter into his glory?" Then beginning with Moses and all the prophets, he interpreted to them the things about himself in all the scriptures.

As they came near the village to which they were going, he walked ahead as if he were going on. But they urged him strongly, saying, "Stay with us, because it is almost evening and the day is now nearly over." So he went in to stay with them. When he was at the table with them, he took bread, blessed and broke it, and gave it to them. Then their eyes were opened, and they recognized him; and he vanished from their sight. They said to each other, "Were not our hearts burning within us while he was talking to us on the road?"[55]

This is the first recorded appearance of the risen Jesus. He has a new resurrection body, which has a crucial continuity with the old one, but is importantly different from it: it is somehow *supplemented*; it is more solid than the stuff of which the current universe is made. It passes through walls; his resurrected neurons fizz. It is a supra-sensual body, designed to be able to glory in the multidimensional pleasures of the new heaven and the new earth, married as they are in him. And the very first thing he chooses to do with it is to go for a walk.

At the Benedictine monastery of Santo Domingo de Silos, on the road to Santiago de Compostela, there is a carved panel depicting the Emmaus road encounter. Christ is shown carrying a pilgrim's satchel. On the satchel is the scallop shell—the ancient sign of the Santiago pilgrim. The craftsman had understood quite a lot.

It is a deep irony—but ironies are so common in the Bible they're actually the norm—that this nomadic God should write the final chapter he does. The chapter ends with an apparent and dramatic change of heart on the part of God. For millennia he has been steadfastly and emphatically against cities. Yet right at the end, he says not only that he is going to build a city, but also that everyone is going to live there.

The picture of the New Jerusalem in the book of Revelation is every nomad's nightmare. It is a vast, glittering, crowded cube, where there is no soft night.[56] It doesn't seem like a place for nuance, for whispering, for respectful tea, or for poems. And I suppose that is how it should be. Why lust after those tantalizing hints of joy that keep us alive now, when Joy himself is there? Why read a poem that ham-fistedly sketches the outline of a lover, when the Lover herself lies beckoning on the bed? By then our appetites will have been redeemed. Our most frantic lusts here will be magnified immeasurably and transformed unimaginably. With those brave new resurrection bodies, we will be sensually satiated in ways that make our most deliciously lurid dreams of sex, food, relationship, music, and understanding seem like the flat, anemic pictures in a washing machine brochure.[57]

Yahweh has not changed his mind. He has not decided that he likes suits and sidewalks. The desert nomad need not worry. The suits will be burned; the sidewalks will ripple like the dune. All that the nomad held precious is there; indeed it is hugely more itself than it was. He loved the stars, but perhaps didn't know in the Hejaz that he loved them because they told him the person who had flung them into space loved him. He will know that love in every way now. At the core of him was his love of community; with his fellows, with the crass, belching strangers who came to his tent; with the thrushes that jumped around his fire in the morning. He loved the road because it honored and enabled that community. He hated the city because it brutalized and suffocated it. But community itself has been redeemed; relationship has been redeemed. That is the meaning of the new city. It's not that true fellowship of the road can somehow manage to exist within the Holy City; there is nowhere else that it can be what it has always really been.

And that is the end of all pilgrimage. There is no other end. "The Spirit and the bride say, 'Come.'"[58]

5

WHY GO? GETTING RID OF JUNK

We went on our pilgrimage
At the blast of the whistling wind
To obtain forgiveness of our sins.
There is the cause of asking.

—"The Voyage of the Ui Chorra"[1]

I was fed up. A relationship was in tatters, and with it all the plans for newness. My work had stopped frightening and therefore exciting me. I let deadlines loom dangerously, just to get a bit of a thrill. As if from a long way away, I heard my friends being faithful and supportive and translated it as being dull, predictable, and intrusive. I ran hard around the park in the very early morning, carrying a knapsack full of encyclopedias, because pain is one of the few things that never loses its novelty. In the evening I chased women, read Graham Greene, and looked at pictures of surf.

"You should go around the world," said the more distant friends when the problem was precisely that I had been.

"You should plan a bank robbery," said the wiser ones.

In fact I went to Charing Cross station and caught the first train out. It went to Sandwich on the Kent coast. That was unfortunate; there were some memories there on the painful side of wistful.

I started to walk to nowhere in particular. Sea fog blew in, turned to rain, and dropped on me. A notice on a gate said, "No entry," so I went through. A track made of gravel and gulls' bones led down to the beach. In this part of England, it is not clear where the land ends and the sea starts. The land and the sea are constantly and inconclusively negotiating. Eventually it seemed clear that I was in the sea. I couldn't be wetter, so I took off all my clothes and ran out a long way toward France until the sea was deep enough to take me. The sky-water poured into the sea, and the sea spat and breathed it back. I put my head under and heard the rub of the water against the sand. "I'll be sand soon," I shouted to no one and started to laugh. And then the sand began to rub something off me.

That night I slept on the dunes beneath some plastic fertilizer bags. I was woken in the early hours by a scavenging fox, and then by the heat of the sun on the back of my neck. I ate an old bread roll, drank from the stream that snaked through the sand, and threw my diary into the sea. I was beginning to learn again how to be happy.

I didn't wash, except in the sea, for a week. I wanted the sand to chafe away whatever was stopping me from feeling. By a very roundabout route (it should have taken a day by a direct march), I walked toward Canterbury. I slept in woods, cabbage fields, and on beaches. If I approached a settlement, I squeezed through a hedge and walked miles to avoid it. I bought tinned fish, chocolate, and beer in garages, because they were anonymous places. You could rely on the cashier to be surly. At a village shop in kind Kent, the owner would have tried to mother me. I convinced myself that I had learned a few words of gull language.

After a week I saw the towers of Canterbury Cathedral rising ahead. I had seen them before and had turned around for yet another detour. But this time I thought I should go. I thought I would shuffle around the cathedral, eat a bun, and catch the train back.

Outside the cathedral I put my foot in a hole, turned my ankle, and fell to the ground with a histrionic scream. I had sprained my ankle. I clearly wasn't meant to go to the sanctuary of St. Thomas, so I caught a cab back to the station.

I didn't need to see St. Thomas. There was nothing I had to leave urgently with him. The sand had rubbed off the worst of the encrusting dross. There was a meandering trail of scurf—a sort of spiritual dandruff—leading all the way back to the first beach.

Many have taken to the road, hoping that the journey will scrape off the spiritual and psychological junk. Sometimes there have been explicit ecclesiastical assurances that it will.

The fourteenth-century bishop, Hamo de Hette, was an orderly man who believed in transparent tariffs. He compiled penitential tables. For a layman, adultery would cost annual pilgrimages for six years to Canterbury, Hereford, Bury St. Edmunds, and Chichester, almsgiving along the way, and the donation each year for six years of a three-pound candle. Clerics seemed to get much better value: one pilgrimage to Walsingham, with almsgiving of six shillings and eight pence en route, would see them right.

When the pilgrimage industry to the Holy Land was in full swing, the system of indulgences was nicely structured. To William Wey, a fifteenth-century pilgrim, is (wrongly) attributed *The Way to Jerusalem*, a guide that helpfully marks the places where indulgences may be granted. He wrote,

> "Ye shall understand that where ye find the sign of the cross
> is plenary remission *a poena et culpa*, and other places, where
> the sign of the cross is not, are seven years and seven Lents
> of indulgence, and the said indulgence was granted of Saint
> Sylvester at the instance of the prayer of Constantine, the
> Emperor, and St. Helena, his mother."[2]

By the mid-fourteenth century, St. Peter's Basilica in Rome was a marketplace, busily peddling remissions. Each of the many altars had its own special relic, and each offered its own particular strength of indulgence. It was a sort of purgatorial capitalism, in which each relic competed for customers. At the top of the pecking order was the Sudarium—the cloth allegedly used by Veronica to wipe the sweat from the face of Jesus as he carried the cross to Calvary, and which was miraculously imprinted with his face. Every hour spent praying before the Sudarium, said the Vatican, meant twelve thousand years off Purgatory. But that meant that the Sudarium chapel was crowded. Market conditions might mean that you'd get better value per visit to the Basilica by praying in some of the more accessible chapels. The arithmetic was sometimes complex.

It must be wonderful to have such certainty. "You can," says the Reformer, "and you don't have to go to a shrine for it. You have been washed in the blood of the Lamb. Know it." Well, yes, but I would often like someone else to take responsibility for my eternal destiny. "You don't understand," says the Roman Catholic Church. "This has nothing to do with salvation. Indulgences are to do with remission of the temporal punishment in Purgatory imposed because of sins that have already been forgiven." Well, yes, I know. The doctrine of purgatory has tremendous psychological appeal. So does the notion that someone in Rome can determine my sentence there.

A couple of months ago I stood, and my son played irreverently, at the foot of the Scala Sancta in Rome—the Holy Staircase, allegedly brought to Rome from Jerusalem by

Helena in the fourth century, and which is thought by the faithful (almost certainly wrongly) to be the staircase leading to Pilate's Praetorium, up and down which Jesus walked on his way to and from his show trial. It is one of the main pilgrimage destinations in Rome and has been for at least many hundreds of years.

It was rush hour on the Scala Sancta. It was crowded with penitents, ascending the steps on their knees—some weeping, some looking nonspecifically miserable, and some briskly businesslike, dexterously clacking their rosaries like pre-Silicon Age Chinese children on their abacuses. Indeed there was a clinical aura of calculation about the whole place. It was not surprising. Pope Pius VII in 1817 declared that each step gave nine years' remission from Purgatory. He was trumped in 1908 by Pope Pius X, who offered a plenary indulgence to everyone who climbed the steps with due reverence after confession and communion. All this brings out the lawyer in me: Which one of the two was right? Isn't the change in the divine legislation a bit unfair on the penitent, obedient pre-1908 climbers? Or is the 1908 edict retroactive?

I thought of climbing the steps myself but felt that it would be voyeuristic. I wasn't particularly penitent; I just wanted to see if anything apart from sore knees would happen, and to be able to tick it off in my own mental guidebook.

"What are those people doing?" bellowed Tom, age four, as he bolted impiously up the staircase. Puffing, red faced, and apologetic, I dragged him out of the chapel under the outraged gaze of the custodian.

It was a very good question. I didn't really know. We went to a café, Tom had some undeserved ice cream, and I read what Charles Spurgeon had said about the steps:

> Our abhorrence of Popery and everything verging upon it rose to a white heat as we saw how it can lower an intelligent nation to the level of fetish worship, and associate the name of the ever-blessed Jesus with a grovelling idolatry. If our mild milk-and-water Protestants could see Popery with their own eyes, they might have less to say against [Protestant] bigotry; and if those who play at ornate worship could see whither their symbolism tends, they would start back aghast, and adhere henceforth to the severest simplicity. Perhaps Luther would never have become a Reformer had it not been for his visit to Rome and his ascent of these very stairs. In the city where he expected to find the church of God in all its holiness, he found sin rampant beyond all precedent. "It is almost incredible," says he, "what infamous actions are committed at Rome; one would require to see it and hear it in order to believe it. It is an ordinary saying that if there is a hell, Rome is built upon it. It is an abyss from whence all sins proceed.[3]

I'm glad I read this. Nothing that inspires bile like that can be all bad. The bile acted on my eyes as Jesus' spit acted on the eyes of the man born blind. It made me look much more sympathetically at everything I saw at the Scala Sancta.

I saw that the penitents knew and practiced something I did not. They knew that what they did with their bodies affected other parts of them. The reason I didn't get down on my knees was complex, but at its root was the corrosive gnostic premise that religion was about my spirit, and my knees—being composed of bone, muscle, and cartilage—weren't relevant to my spirit.

"Fetish worship"? Because they climb a staircase of dubious historicity? Hardly. We all worship our own synthetic images of God. Growing Christian maturity simply means that the images become incrementally less inadequate. "[God] is the great iconoclast," C. S. Lewis truly wrote.[4] He is constantly smashing up the images we have of him. And anyway, no one is in any danger of confusing God with a staircase or a saint's mummified head. There's a real and malignant danger of confusing God with the things that Scripture says about him.

Those step-climbers had, too, a desperation that I would do well to emulate: to be rid of stuff.

It is too easy, when modern Protestant readers thumb through the old pilgrimage accounts, to get up such a head of Lutheran steam over the question of indulgences that you can't see anything else. If that's a problem, I suggest that you put indulgences into a hermetically sealed box from which they can't crawl out. Label that box, as you please, either "Psychologically helpful but theologically unorthodox" or "Incomprehensible" and move on to get the most out of the rest of the story. For both the old and the new stories are worth telling.

"I went on pilgrimage," said Martin, a forty-something computer programmer from Heidelberg with a taste for the sterner passages in Leviticus, "because I wanted to leave behind the pain of a wrecked marriage."

"I went on pilgrimage," said Martha, a fragrant, very English lady of indeterminate age with a taste for very dry sherry, who had sold her Chelsea flat with its Thames view and walked with her poodle from Calais to Santiago, "because I hated my desk and everything that was on it. I wanted to leave the humdrum behind. I wanted to leave a world where nothing happened, and stride (okay, totter) into a world of possibility."

"Pilgrimage makes us vulnerable and different," said Father Edward Murphy, a Roman Catholic priest based at the Yugoslavian shrine of Medujorge. "It gives us the freedom to step out of the ordinary and do something heroic and also to empty ourselves completely."[5]

"The feet of the wanderer are like the flower," said Aitareya Brahmana, "his soul growing and reaping the fruit; and all his sins are destroyed by his fatigues in wandering. Therefore wander."[6]

The same language recurs throughout the millennia. Leaving things behind. Destroying things. Going to new places where a new start can be made. Becoming a different person. Vomiting out the old. Sloughing off old skins.

There are three stages at which you can leave things behind: at the very beginning (where you are leaving behind the things at home that stop you from being the person you should be); in the course of the journey (as the abrasion of the road rubs away some of the stuff that cakes onto us all); and at the end (where the burden is thrown off at the feet of a saint, a holy stone, or a newly realized idea).

Were Martin and Martha contemptible cowards? Should they have stayed behind, facing manfully the things they so feared?

There's nothing necessarily contemptible about cowardice. It is a much-underrated Christian virtue. "Keep your way far from [the immoral woman]," urges Proverbs, "and do not go near the door of her house"[7]—don't confront her and risk ending up in her bed. When Potiphar's wife urged Joseph to sleep with her, Joseph didn't pray or preach; he fled.[8] There are some sorts of temptation that human beings are constitutionally bad at resisting. They are, unsurprisingly, the temptations that cut at the very root of what we are. We are quintessentially relational creatures, and so anonymous, nonrelational sex is particularly attractive. We are migratory animals, so inertia will snap at our heels throughout our lives. To stop a wandering creature from wandering is a great demonic coup; lots of other sins will come trotting meekly in the wake of inertia. So run. Get out on the road. That desk is dangerous. "Flee the wrath to come," screams the sign from a nearby church that nobody ever seems to go to. "Flee the wrath that comes from staying wherever it is you are," say I. The best way of moving on from that shattered relationship is to move on from one village to the next. We are incurably metaphorical creatures, as mind-body-spirit unities are bound to be. We are curiously calibrated. The distance in miles from that deadly desk is read as the distance our soul has moved from everything the desk represents.

But the universe is even more helpful to the pilgrim than that. Gravity and magnetism are governed by a cubic law. The power of a magnetic field diminishes in proportion to the cube of the distance from the center. Move three feet away, and the field will be nine times weaker than at the center. And so on. It's mercifully the same with pilgrimage. The metaphysical calculus is kind and impressive. Every step from the desk takes the pilgrim much further than you'd think from the desk's power.

There is nothing cowardly about leaving something where there is nothing, to go somewhere where there is something. Someone who leaves a burning town, after he's done his best to save others from it, is simply prudent. By all means come back later to help in the reconstruction, if that's an option, but if the town ought to be abandoned, the coward is the one who sits weeping in the smoldering remains, unable to leave the memories of a vanished life.

There is nothing cowardly about embracing the new. Normally it's the other way around: the cowards are the conservatives—the ones who are terrified of sights other than the ones they are used to seeing; the ones who find life unimaginable without the pillars of the office, the comforting church, the anniversaries, and the eight o' clock TV soap. Of course, there will be exceptions. Sometimes the really sturdy adventurer will stay to face the crashing waves of an ill parent or a disabled child. But the qualities of those stayers are the qualities of the road-taker, not those of the comfortable suburbanite. The anthropological and divine norm, remember, is to travel. We're wired to expect, at every level of our being, a new sight every second, with every step. The challenge of this book is to dare to be normal. Very few people are. It is thrilling, and it's not the coward's way of dealing with life.

"Whoever comes to me and does not hate father and mother, wife and children, brothers and sisters, yes, and even life itself, cannot be my disciple" said Jesus.[9] There may be some rabbinic hyperbole there, and it is certainly not a mandate for callous abandonment of our responsibilities, but we can't write it out of the Bible. "Leaving," in the context in which Jesus spoke, meant precisely, literally that. It meant taking to the road with him, becoming, as he was, a homeless tramp. And in that there was and is great joy. In modern New Age writing, the object of pilgrimage is often described as "finding yourself." "Know thyself" was the Socratic maxim at the mountain sanctuary of Delphi, one of the most ancient pilgrimage destinations. If you're Christian, don't be too sniffily dismissive of that sort of language. The church could do with more Christians who have found themselves. After all, Jesus promised that he who lost his life would "find it,"[10] and that was presumably a good thing. I have met a few people who have found themselves. You can see the glow a mile away, and people are drawn to it like moths.

Yes, there is a cost. Count it. If your calculation says that it is too high, go back to your desk and your mall. But you've got your math wrong. Just go. Knock the dust of the old life off your shoes, and start walking. And don't look over your shoulder; it can be dangerous, as Lot's wife found.

One very significant thing is left behind immediately—your old status as a non-pilgrim. You "come out" as a seeker. You leave behind your non-seekerishness. You are immediately different in your own eyes and in the eyes of everyone who knows you. If you have announced that you are going on pilgrimage and in fact do nothing but sit in your bedroom, staring at the wall, things will never be the same again. You're branded. That is helpful.

Then begins the second kind of leaving behind: the sloughing off en route, by the benevolent attrition of the tarmac, of the accumulated dross of the decades. "Something needed to change inside me to equip me for a new life," wrote an English woman who walked to Santiago de Compostela. "Solitude coupled with the regular rhythm of walking is cleansing, therapeutic."[11] That is fairly typical.

"It just goes to show what a bit of fresh air and sunshine can do," said Jim, a Glasgow Presbyterian. "Everyone feels better after they've taken the dog for a walk. To call that a 'spiritual experience' is nonsense. It devalues the whole currency of Christian language. Nothing is a 'spiritual experience' unless it involves True Repentance and Belief in the Gospel." He spat out the capital letters; they were obviously meant to indicate sacredly technical terms.

I did not know where to start with Jim. And so I didn't. I didn't need to. He was about to set out, in the company of some supremely nice, altruistic Buddhists, on a three-day hike to a Celtic stone cross in a rowan grove on the west coast of Scotland. He sent me a text on day two: "Simply being alive as a human being is necessarily a religious experience, isn't it? Why didn't you tell me before?" He still believed in the necessity of repentance and belief in the gospel, and so do I.

"Travel is fatal to prejudice, bigotry and narrow-mindedness," declared Mark Twain.[12] And he was right. No one is a sectarian at the end of the road to Santiago. It is only possible to hate those we don't understand, and it is hard to hate those we don't understand but who have lent us their water bottles.

You get rid of lots of lies. Your body and your workmates tell you that you can't walk twenty-five miles a day. They are wrong; you can. Your body tells you that you won't be able to do without the customary eleven o'clock Starbucks latte. It's lying; you can. Your upbringing tells you that you'd never be able to be moved by the elaborate procession of a statue of the Virgin around a Pyrenean village, or sleep on the ground, or undress in a dormitory in front of dozens of other pilgrims, or eat rams' testicles. But you can. So even if you have no great epiphany on the way, there's a lot more truth in your life than there was.

As for epiphany, if you want to remain unchanged, be very careful. There's no such thing as a person to whom "those sorts of things don't happen." Here is a passage from the Indian notebook of a very prosaic and very young Cambridge student, who was walking along a track in the foothills of the Himalayas, minding his own business:

> In a sudden explosion of light in the air over the trees a pair of swifts screamed for a long moment, and seemed for that moment to be stuck to the sky: unchanging in every detail, but moving as fast as ever before; immutable, but without the stiffness of a silhouette; lent a new fluidity by the fact of unchangeableness. Then a gust nudged a cloud on and the light was gone; the swifts angled and dived below the parapet of a farm. I knew then, as Peter Matthiessen put it, that "all names fall short of the shining of things," but this was an old lesson, relearned. That patch of sky over India had a musty, homely smell, like an old exercise book; there should have been inkblots and spelling corrections on it.

I was that student. If I'd had any sense, I'd have learned lessons that day that would have saved me a lot of heartache.

The final kind of leaving behind is what you leave behind finally: what you drop off at the destination. John Bunyan's pilgrim wanted to get rid of the burden on his back.

> "That is that which I seek for," says Christian, "even to be rid of this heavy burden: but get it off myself I cannot, nor is there any man in our country that can take it off my shoulders; therefore am I going this way, as I told you, that I may be rid of my burden.

He lost it at the cross:

> He ran thus till he came at a place somewhat ascending; and upon that place stood a cross, and a little below, in the bottom, a sepulchre. So I saw in my dream, that just as Christian came up with the cross, his burden loosed from off his shoulders, and fell from off his back, and began to tumble, and so continued to do till it came to the mouth of the sepulchre, where it fell in, and I saw it no more. Then was Christian glad and lightsome, and said with a merry heart, "He hath given me rest by his sorrow, and life by his death."[13]

Bunyan was stoutly and emphatically allegorical. And yet the language he used to describe Christian's relief at the loss of his sin and guilt is echoed again and again in pilgrim accounts. "Whatever evil a woman or man has done since birth is all destroyed by just one bath [there]," says the sage Pulastaya in the Mahabharata of the sacred Hindu ford of Pushkara, in Rajahstan.[14] Sikh pilgrims travel to Amritsar, where the Guru is said to have filled a pool with nectar:

> Sing praises to this most sacred of all places dedicated to the Name of God, to the sacred water that banishes all pain and distress. Let all who come here sing its praises. Let them here discover the bliss of mystical union with God. Only those who know true devotion will come, for this is no place for hypocrites and deceivers. Here divine music will be sung, sublimely beautiful music, which will bring joy to all who hear it. Here we will witness wonders; here we will meet the truly devout; here we will find peace.[15]

The fourteenth-century Muslim traveler Ibn Battuta wrote of his arrival in Mecca:

> "May God Most High number us amongst those whose visitation is acceptable, whose merchandise in seeking to perform it brings him gain [in the world to come], whose actions in the cause of God are written [in the Book of Life]

and whose burdens of sin are effaced by the acceptance [of the merit won by the Hajj], through His loving kindness and graciousness."[16]

In the Christian tradition, the psychological relief of having completed the obligation necessary to claim a plenary indulgence was and is overwhelming. At the top of the Scala Sancta, the pilgrims looked lighter than at the bottom. Christian groups from many denominations clog the steep and narrow roads of the Via Dolorosa in Jerusalem (a medieval reconstruction of the route taken by Jesus to Calvary). They often carry a wooden cross with them. "I was desperate to carry that cross," said Pedro, a plumber from Brazil who had sold his van to pay for the flight to Tel Aviv.

But I didn't feel I could push myself forward. I didn't go down to dinner the night before we were to go up the Via Dolorosa. I knelt by my bed all night, asking God for the honor of sharing his shame. At breakfast the priest said, "I think Pedro should take the cross," and I was so happy. It was not heavy, and I am strong, but as I walked I felt all the stupid things I have ever done flowing into that cross. I began to sweat, and I began to be frightened that it—they—would crush me. The people thought I was play-acting. But by the time we came to the Holy Sepulchre I was done in. My knees were jelly. I staggered into the courtyard and collapsed. They clapped, a bit nervously, thinking that I was going slightly too far. But then I got up, and I could have flown. I raised my arms above my head and I sang and laughed and suddenly the world was full of color. The pigeons were rainbow-striped. All those sins were gone—dissolved into those wooden planks. I left my past in Jerusalem.

Other pilgrims leave their crutches; they don't need them anymore. They are often displayed in proud museums at the shrines, testifying to the healing power of the saint. It was commonplace in the Middle Ages for pilgrims to bring effigies of themselves to leave there. Walsingham has a fine collection. Sometimes they left complete statues, which say, as Pedro said, "The old me is here. I'm a newborn babe." A candle of the same weight or height as the pilgrim would sometimes be left burning at a shrine. Sometimes pilgrims left individual body parts—wax, steel, or wooden legs and noses—saying that a very specific prayer had been answered, or as a token of faith that it would be. A shepherd left his necrotic finger on the altar at Durham Cathedral, confident that St. Cuthbert would give him a new one. After visiting the shrine of St. Thomas of Canterbury, a pilgrim coughed up a huge parasitic worm, relieving him of his chronic pain. The grateful patient hung the worm near the shrine.

Medieval Europe clanked as penitential pilgrims shuffled along, sometimes in shackles, sometimes bound with chains made from the weapons they had used to kill or wound their victims. It is said that those chains sometimes evaporated when they came to the shrine of the saint they had been traveling to see. I see no reason to doubt it.

Sometimes life itself is left behind at the end of a pilgrimage. Hindu *sannyasis* (holy men) spend their lives wandering, begging, across the holy body of the goddess, the land of India. When they feel death approach, they go on a very special pilgrimage to a place where they know they can be quiet and composed. Many in all traditions have done the same. "Alone in my little hut without a human being in my company," goes the poem of an Irish Christian hermit, "dear has been my pilgrimage before going to meet my death."[17] And the mouse Reepicheep, remember, in C. S. Lewis's *Voyage of the Dawn Treader*, sets off alone in his coracle, thrilled at the thought of finding out what happens at the edge of the world, and knowing that he will never return. We last see him as his coracle rushes up and over a green wave, "and since that moment no one can truly claim to have seen Reepicheep the Mouse. But my belief is that he came safe to Aslan's country and is alive there to this day."[18]

When you reel out of the hospital having received your terminal diagnosis, you could do a lot worse than to kiss your family good-bye, carry your kayak down to the sea, and paddle out to meet salvation. But that might be selfish and cowardly. Perhaps you should surf into the light on a morphine high, holding your wife's hand. Either way, however unconscious you've been of the journey of life, you'll know then that you're traveling.

Are sins scraped off? Many have thought and felt that they are. No, we don't win our own salvation; it is freely given. But it has to be received. Repentance has to be real to be effective. "If you *truly* seek me, you will surely find me," we're told.[19] So there are some sorts of apparent seeking that don't result in finding. Indeed, as we've already observed, since there are very many apparent seekers, and (we're told) very few finders, most of the apparent seekers aren't seeking at all in the way Jesus meant.

The sort of seeking you must have in order to get off the sofa and walk across Europe is, I'd have thought, more likely to be the real thing than the sort of seeking that makes you dress up in your Sunday suit and drive around the corner to church. The sort of repentance that makes you kneel on the threadbare carpet of a Jerusalem doss-house in the hope that you can carry a lump of wood up a hill is, I'd have thought, more likely to be real repentance than the sort of repentance that gives a nice, cozy feeling at the end of the Sunday service.

Shane Claiborne talks about his Christian upbringing in eastern Tennessee. At evangelistic services, there would be the great call to the front; and every year he and his mates would go forward, singing "Just as I Am"; and each year, he says, they would leave *just as they were*. Whatever your fastidious theological doubts about penitential pilgrimages, that never happened to someone who had walked from Paris to Rome in winter, losing toes from frostbite on the St. Bernard Pass, carrying a yoke forged from the club he'd used to beat his wife to death.

And there is this too. I can feel the scars left by forgiven sins. Sometimes the scar tissue is pathologically exuberant. It interferes with function and needs to be rasped away. All I can say is that the business of putting one foot in front of the other has sometimes done that for me. Does that relate in any way to the doctrine of Purgatory? I don't know, and I'm not hugely interested. C. S. Lewis, at any rate, thought that there was a lot to commend the idea of Purgatory. Suppose, he suggested, we arrive at the heavenly gates. St. Peter greets us. There is no doubt about our right to enter: that right was given by the grace of the Lord. "You can come in," says St. Peter, "but (sorry to mention it), you still smell a bit, and your clothes need some attention. There's a rather bracingly cold bath here, and a clean set of clothes." Would we want to go unwashed through the gates? asked Lewis. And he expected the answer no. Purgatory for him was another form of grace.[20] And remember that in Dante the gate of Purgatory is reached *after* the gate of Paradise.

This theme of washing before arrival in the pilgrimage destination is ubiquitous. Muslims undergo elaborate washing rituals, cut their hair, shave, and abandon all personal adornment before they enter Mecca. Hindu pilgrims to the shrine of Sabarimalai take a vow of austerity forty-five to sixty days before they set out.

It lasts throughout the journey. They have no sex and no female company; they eat no meat or eggs, drink no alcohol, wear no shoes, take only two changes of clothes (all in plain blue, black, or ochre), bite their tongues when they are tempted to abuse others, and have three baths a day.

"Who shall ascend the hill of the LORD?" asks the psalmist. "And who shall stand in his holy place? Those who have clean hands and pure hearts, who do not lift up their souls to what is false, and do not swear deceitfully."[21] It is not only what we're told to do, but also what we feel we should do. And why is that? Often the fact that we reach (in my case very unusually) for the soap before we get to the pilgrimage destination is the most reliable indicator to ourselves of what the pilgrimage is really all about. It is because pilgrimage is about an *encounter*, and we want to look and smell our best.

6

WHY GO?
THIRST FOR AN ENCOUNTER

It is time for me to pass from the shelter of a habitation.

To journey as a pilgrim over the waves of the bold and splendid sea . . .

Time to deliberate how I may find the great Son of Mary.

—CELEDABHAILL [1]

A longing for God set on fire the heart of this most blessed nun, Egeria.

In the strength of the glorious Lord, she fearlessly set out on an immense

journey to the other side of the world.

—VALERIUS [2]

When the sweet showers of April fall and shoot

Down through the drought of March to pierce the root,

Bathing every vein in liquid power

From which there springs the engendering of the flower . . .

Then people long to go on pilgrimages

And palmers long to seek the stranger strands

Of far-off saints, hallowed in sundry lands,

And specially, from every shire's end

In England, down to Canterbury they wend
To seek the holy blissful martyr, quick
In giving help to them when they were sick.

—GEOFFREY CHAUCER [3]

IT WAS A TYPICAL DAY IN THE OLD CITY OF JERUSALEM. The souk was as aromatic as ever; the cheerfulness of the olive-wood camel sellers was the perennial triumph of hope over experience and bookkeeping; Israeli soldiers lolled and chewed; priests in billowing robes sailed down the steep roads like black tea-clippers; the crowds parted before them like the Red Sea before Moses; T-shirts read, "I got stoned in the Gaza Strip" and "Uzi does it," and nobody laughed at them anymore.

The tourists fulfilled, absurdly, all the national stereotypes. Being abroad accentuates national characteristics. Not every woman in Tokyo wears pop-socks and baseball boots, but this lot did. The Americans wore golfing checks and thought that raising the volume could make anyone understand their English. I sweated in a completely inappropriate tweed jacket and shoes built for a grouse moor.

The baseball boots padded along Muristan Road, following a rising sun flag toward the Holy Sepulchre. I had nothing else to do, so I loped after them. They each had a blue plastic clipboard and a pen. As they walked around, they ticked things off. There is the place where Jesus died: tick. There, where the women are wailing, is where they laid out and anointed his body: tick. Just around the corner is the tomb that couldn't hold him, where the universe was changed forever: tick.

"What is the point of all that?" asked another man in a tweed jacket. "They will creep back onto the 747, creep back to their little prefabricated boxes, download their identical and identically non-understood photos onto their PCs, file their clipboards, and go back to work as uncomplaining wage-slaves for huge multinationals." A passing priest wafted some incense from a silver censer into his face. He coughed and stopped.

"You're too cynical," I said. "Humans are porous animals—spiritual sponges. They're drenched in sanctity here. Watch this." I tapped one of the Japanese tourists on the shoulder and asked him if he spoke English. He did.

"Do you mind me asking?" I ventured. "You've obviously come a long way to get here. What does it mean to you? Will it change you at all?"

"I'm changed very much," he said.

I looked smugly back to the tweed jacket.

"Go on."

"I got very bad diarrhea from the pickles, and I have lost

two kilos." He turned back to his checklist and adjusted the flash settings on his Nikon.

I want very much to believe that every tourist is at least in part a pilgrim, but the evidence is against it. Every pilgrim with a brain is at least in part a tourist, but that's not at all the same thing. Every pilgrim is *interested* in seeing where it all happened. Many seek the faith-building reassurance that can come from knowing that there was indeed a pool at Bethesda or a town called Emmaus about eight miles from Jerusalem, although, as we will see, seeing those things more often shakes faith exhilaratingly up instead of consolidating it in the expected way. But what sets the pilgrim apart from the list-ticker is that he hopes, and at some level believes, that someone will hear his footsteps coming from afar, and as he approaches the threshold, that person will open the door and bid him come in and eat. The pilgrim probably has no very clear idea about what that person will look like; but he knows that when the door is opened, there will be an ecstasy of mutual recognition, that it will be home, and that from inside will come music that he has heard somewhere before—music that he was desperate to hear again and that was the siren song that called him to whatever Jerusalem he's in.

One of the shocking things that has to be faced is that many of the pilgrims who have sought and continue to seek that sort of sublime appointment do so by visiting boxes of decaying body parts and other ecclesiastical rubble.

After disgracing himself at Scala Sancta, Tom assured me that he had turned from his evil ways, and so we went on to Santa Croce in Gerusalemme—the modern relic-hunter's paradise. It was to Santa Croce that St. Helena brought several pieces of the True Cross found in Jerusalem. Several other relics joined it.

The floor of the nave of Santa Croce is just about original: colorful, rough mosaic, scuffed by thousands of faithful feet, beautifully at odds with the barbaric Baroque of the rest of the church. Why should anyone think that Baroque expounded Christianity better than the rustic floor? The floor is like the road that brought the pilgrims to Rome, but rearranged in kabbalistic spirals and shot through with the colors of deep earth.

In the aisles are dramatic oil paintings: St. Bernard miraculously extracts a tooth from the relic of St. Cesarius; St. Bernard of Clairvaux induces the antipope Victor IV to humble himself before Pope Innocent II. Innocent has an embryonic, evolving halo. A shaven-headed, hook-nosed priest in black and white sat in a pew, watching me take notes. His face was like the stone skull above him. Dust danced. And that, I suppose, was the whole message of the place.

The chapel of the relics is up a grand marble staircase. "The idea that permeates [the approach]" said the badly translated notice, "is that of the pilgrimage to the Calvary, musing over the mystery of the Passion and the Death of Jesus." Tom didn't muse. He galloped.

The church holds three fragments from the Cross, one of the nails that pierced Jesus (12.5 centimeters long, with a square stem), the "Titulus" (part of the sign fixed to the cross that told onlookers who they were seeing), two thorns from the crown (one 3.5 centimeters long, the other 3.4 centimeters), the index finger of St. Thomas (which, if genuine, I suppose has a 50 percent chance of being the one that reached out to explore the wound in the side of the risen Jesus), a piece of the good thief's cross, and three fragments of stone from the column of the scourging.

The devotees at the reliquaries didn't know quite where their curiosity ended and their devotion began. They were slightly embarrassed by their curiosity. If they saw you looking at them, they would look deliberately and emphatically away at something else, like men caught surveying the top shelf at the newsagent.

"Tell me what to do with all this stuff and all this feeling," I pleaded with Mandy, a very religious Roman Catholic living a consecrated life in Milan.

"I really don't know," she said, "but I'm worried that you're going to write this up as if it were a mainspring of Catholic devotion."

Her embarrassment, viewed historically, was strange. The veneration of relics has a long and important history. It is impossible to disentangle that history from the history of pilgrimage itself.

When Roman soldiers murdered St. Vincent (c. 304), Christians swooped in like crows to dip their clothes in his blood. When Polycarp was martyred in Smyrna in 155, his fellows triumphantly noted, "We recovered his bones, rarer than gold and more precious than costly jewels. We laid them in a fitting place."[4] When Henry's knights butchered Thomas in Canterbury in 1170, bystanders scraped his brains into bowls and wiped their eyes with cloth smeared with his gore.

And that was the general pattern. Holy people were quickly dismembered and distributed—a trade hugely boosted by the AD 787 decree of the Second Nicene Council that no altar was complete without a relic. Of course there was abuse: throughout the Middle Ages there was a lucrative trade in bogus relics and plenty of contemporary cynicism. The inveterate sixteenth-century traveler Dr. Andrew Boorde, known to history and the inns en route to Rome and Santiago as "Merry Andrew," assured the readers of his Continental pilgrims' guidebook that "there is not one hair or bone of St. James in Compostela . . . but only the sickle and hooke which [they said] dyd saw and cutte off the head of St. James."[5] Chaucer's Pardoner passes off pig bones as the relics of a saint, and a pillowcase as the veil of the Virgin. Abbot Guibert of Nogent spoke of a relic-hawker trying to sell a piece of the bread chewed by Jesus at the Last Supper. Probably only the most audacious sold, and the very dim bought, glass vials containing the exhaled breath of Christ.

The abuse was tactically very useful to the Reformers,

who denounced relic veneration as idolatry and superstition. That most subtle and bookish of the Reformers, Erasmus, was appalled by what he found when he went to Canterbury in 1515 with his friend Colet. There was quite a museum there, containing the sacred rust from the sword that hacked Thomas à Becket to death, the skull of the saint (covered in silver, but for the forehead, left bare to be kissed), a fragment of linen used by Becket "to wipe the perspiration from his face or his neck, the runnings from his nose, or such other superfluities from which the human frame is not free," and in the crypt, the remains of other holy men: "sculls, jawbones, teeth, hands, fingers, entire arms." The last straw came when Colet was expected to kiss an arm that "still had the bloody flesh adhering to it." Colet could not steel himself to the job, and the two went off fulminating, more devoted Reformers than they had arrived.[6] It was not good marketing by the Roman church.

Many of the Protestant readers of this book will share Erasmus and Colet's distaste for the practice of relic veneration, and they will articulate their distaste theologically in the same way. But any truly biblical theology has to deal more sympathetically with relics than Oliver Cromwell's rampaging, vandalizing Roundheads did.

"Elisha died, and they buried him. Now bands of Moabites used to invade the land in the spring of the year. As a man was being buried, a marauding band was seen and the man was thrown into the grave of Elisha; as soon as the man touched the bones of Elisha, he came to life and stood on his feet."[7] It is a spectacular relic-related miracle of the sort beloved of the Middle Ages and loathed by the Reformers—the sort of miracle that would have founded a cathedral and kept a huge economy throbbing. And it's not just the Old Testament: "God did extraordinary miracles through Paul," we're told. No problem there: we're happy to hear that any Sunday morning. But it doesn't stop there. It continues, "so that when the handkerchiefs or aprons that had touched his skin were brought to the sick, their diseases left them, and the evil spirits came out of them."[8]

What is going on? There is, in all the mainstream religions, and deep in the human heart, a desire to touch and to be touched. Go to the Topkapi Palace in Istanbul and you will see (if it's Ramadan and you are allowed to the special enclosure where they are kept) the staff of Moses and a hair from the beard of the prophet Mohammed. Ibn Battuta, arriving in Medina, describes how he "prayed in the illustrious garden between the tomb of the Prophet and the noble pulpit, and reverently touched the fragment that remains of the palm trunk against which the Prophet stood when he preached."[9] Many a temple contains a hair, fingernail, or toe bone of the Buddha, in direct contravention of his own prohibition of relics. When the Tantric Buddhist tulku Dudjom Rinpoche died in France in 1987, his corpse was mummified and flown to Nepal, where, peering sightlessly through a glass window, it presides over the business of a mountain stupa. The practice of kissing the True Cross in Jerusalem had to be policed rigorously because cunning pilgrims bit pieces off and were gradually gnawing away the most sacred relic of all. In the Christian Middle Ages, architects designed saints' tombs with openings in them through which pilgrims could lower strips of cloth—*brandea*—to touch the relic, or with arches beneath, so that pilgrims could crawl in and feel themselves enfolded by the saint. Christian pilgrims swept the dust from the tombs of saints, mixed it with water, and drank it. In Canterbury the "Water of St. Thomas"—a few drops of the saint's blood mixed with gallons of water—was thought to be a panacea for all human woes.

It is fashionable to dismiss all this, and the healings and transformations that go with it, as hysteria, as if that explained anything. But all that can accurately be said is that the devotees of the relics desperately wanted a relationship with the saint, because the saint had some sort of special connection with the holy. In the Apostles' Creed, we mumble unthinkingly, "I believe . . . in the communion of the saints," and then leave hoping that no one talks to us. But the relic-venerators not only believed in the communion of saints but also drank it. They knew that since we live as physical beings in a physical world, God is fairly likely to choose to communicate with us in physical ways: through the touch of a human being, dead or alive (hence all the New Testamental talk about healing by the laying on of hands, and all the theology associated with the apostolic succession); through the Eucharistic bread and wine; through sacramental sex; and so on.

Who hates the cult of relics most? Why, the gnostics, of

course. And anything that upsets them can't be all bad. I find all the macabre carnival of relic veneration hard to stomach, but wherever relics are at the centre of a cult, gnosticism withers. We should all look a bit harder at the squeamishness that makes us frown at relics. We might well find a little gnostic crouched in the middle of it. Stamp on it, and run gleefully off to Jerusalem, taking in a dead saint on the way if it pleases you, but eating, drinking, and playing with lots of live ones anyway.

Although the Holy Spirit is a predator, he is a gentle predator. He will leap out in ambush to say hello, but not to rape. The encounter that the real pilgrims want won't happen unless you are prepared for it to happen.

I wrote this in my notebook about St. Peter's Basilica in Rome:

> It's a faith-destroying place. To get there you run the gaunt-let of the religious tat-shops: bad plastic models of fat, smug madonnas; grotesquely huge baby Jesuses—presumably genetically modified—with long, flowing, Aryan locks; they would buckle any crib made by man. And there are endless depictions, in Taiwan's finest polyethylene, of the sufferings of Jesus. You can have, within the constraints of Roman crucifix-ion (or the mediaeval view of it), just about any combination you like. You can have the head slumped to the right, or the

left, or raised arrogantly. You can have one or both shoulders dislocated. You can have Mary, in the dress of a Florentine Quattrocento noblewoman or a German nun, clutching the foot of the cross or weeping in a way that does not disturb her mascara. Pope John Paul II is still disproportionately popular on the postcards. He has a kinder face than Benedict. His Papal blessing, usually with a border of spring flowers and prancing lambs, is a big seller.

In the square, the faithful, with real stamina, flood past the mortgage-endangeringly expensive ice creams and paninis towards the holy metal detectors.

A crowd has gathered around a plastic statue of the Virgin. She has a slight stoop and a used-car salesman's smile. Some are carrying banners saying, *Non tremens*, "Do not fear." They press close. They are almost all women, but not all of them are old. Many press handkerchiefs onto the statue's face. I wonder if they are wiping her tears. Some press rosaries into her hands. They cross themselves repeatedly, and back away, holding her gaze. The Virgin's red heart is externalised—marsupialised. I am not moved, except to a cafe down the road.

Nothing happened to me in Rome. How could it? Anyone with the arrogance to write that wouldn't have known Jesus if he'd come up and asked me for the price of a bed at a homeless hostel, which, come to think of it, he did. "The truth knocks on the door," wrote Robert Pirsig, "and you say, 'Go away, I'm looking for the truth.' And so it goes away."[10]

I left the baseball-booted Japanese at the Holy Sepulchre and wound my way toward the Western Wall. Just off the main square of the Jewish Quarter, I sat down to drink coffee and watch a commotion.

A tidy American in his early thirties, dressed in white robes made from bedsheets, had climbed on a chair and started to denounce his listeners in biblical terms (King James Version). "Ye are serpents," he told a group of giggling eight-year-olds. "Ye are a generation of vipers. How can ye escape the damnation of hell?"

"You are chaff," he shouted to an old woman whose Auschwitz number was still tattooed into her forearm. "He is coming, I tell ye, who will thoroughly purge his floor, and gather his wheat into the garner; but he will burn up the chaff with unquenchable fire."

Some young paratroopers darted behind him and lifted up his robe. He was wearing tight blue underpants. He looked delighted, as if this was confirmation of his ministry. He turned to them with a smile of unshakable confidence: "Go on, for therefore saith the wisdom of God, I will send them prophets and apostles, and some of them they shall slay and persecute."

The police arrived, along with a bookish man with round glasses and a doctor's bag. The prophet was coaxed down from his chair, led to a waiting van, and driven off to the K'far Shmuel psychiatric hospital, where they have made this type of case something of a specialty. They would write on the notes, "Jerusalem Syndrome."

It is a fascinating and complex condition.[11] It occurs almost always in Western Protestants of a conservative, Bible-believing background, and it generally happens like this. Someone very religious comes to Jerusalem for the first time. In his head are many pictures of Jerusalem. They are bequests from childhood, when the family read the Bible around the dinner table, and they are his most treasured possessions. They are so fundamental to him that he cannot distinguish them from his own personality. His expectations of Jerusalem are immense. He is the classic religious pilgrim, seeking an encounter with the God he worships. But the moment he lands at Ben Gurion airport, things start to go wrong. Of course he never consciously expected the Israeli airport staff to be blowing shofars or wearing phylacteries, but all the same, at some level of his unconscious, a little seed of discord is sown. It starts to grow as he climbs onto an air-conditioned bus, rather than a chariot, to take him up the fast metaled road to Jerusalem. When he sees the lights of the Holy City, the panic mounts. There are traffic cops, burger joints, and chain stores, and no camels anywhere.

From his hotel room he can see the Old City of Jerusalem, which contains the holiest sites of Christendom. But it is night, and all he can really make out is the golden Dome of the Rock on the Temple Mount. It suddenly dawns on him that the iconic monument of Jerusalem is a mosque.

The next morning the tour group, after prayers led by their pastor, heads straight to the Old City. Unlike some more cautious Protestants, this group has decided to go to the Church of the Holy Sepulchre, rather than to pretend that the much more authentic-looking but almost certainly inauthentic Garden Tomb is the real site.

At the Holy Sepulchre, the patient begins to show signs of real distress. None of his beloved pictures look anything like this. There is no green hill outside the city wall. Where the three crosses stood is an elaborate gilded altar policed by frowning priests from Mount Athos. The tomb isn't in a garden but is inside a monstrous edicule. Piety is suffocated by incense and body odor.

The patient reels out in a daze. He sees Catholics carrying a cross to the church and wonders what on earth Christianity has to do with them. The Garden of Gethsemane looks more as it should—at least there are trees there—but an afternoon trip to the City of David does terrible damage. This tiny, grubby little patch of land was the Jerusalem spoken of by much of the Old Testament? David looked down lustfully onto Bathsheba from a house like that, rather than from a glittering, capacious palace? Isn't God supposed to have painted on a much bigger canvas than that? The Valley of the Shadow of Death is full of abandoned refrigerators and piles of human dung.

He is quiet at dinner. He creeps away to his room soon

afterward and opens his Bible. That makes it worse. He doesn't sleep. The next day, he makes his excuses and doesn't join the rest of the party. He spends the day obsessively washing, cutting his fingernails, and shaving his body hair. He throws all his old clothes into the bin and rips up his sheets to make robes. At dawn the next morning he strides out, barefoot, to begin his ministry.

This is a classic case of "cognitive dissonance." The ideas or pictures so long cherished are emphatically contradicted by reality. The rational thing to do would be to alter the ideas and pictures. But that is impossible. There is too much emotional investment in them. They are inextricably woven into who the patient is, and to dissect them out would be to destroy the patient. So instead, the patient goes the other way. He creates a world in which the pictures are true, a world in which people wear togas and loincloths. And he asserts that he and God know that is real, and anyone who disagrees is deluded and will soon be shown, catastrophically, to be wrong.

We see the same syndrome again and again in conservative religion. The greater the evidence against its assertions, the greater the zeal with which they are preached, the greater the consequent isolation from the rest of the world, and the greater the ease with which the cult members can be protected against the corrupting power of alternative worldviews. A lot of blame can be laid at the door of the expression "faithful remnant." It's easy for congregants not schooled in logic to believe the preachers when they say, "We're a despised remnant, and therefore we must be the truly faithful ones."

What sort of encounter was the patient really seeking? Not, despite his protestations, an encounter with the God of the Bible, but an encounter with the God of his presumptions about the Bible, the God of his own making. That's not relationship; that's masturbation. And one of the very useful things that pilgrimage can do, if it doesn't propel you into a secure unit, is transmute masturbatory fantasy into real relationship.

7

WHERE TO? THIN PLACES

You are here to kneel

Where prayer has been valid.

—T. S. Eliot, *Four Quartets*[1]

And the breeze that comes from it

Is as the honey-bees' first swarming,

A sweet odour over the turf,

Of musk or balm in the midst of the world . . .

The drops of her blood are as the red shower

Of the berries of the wild rose,

The tears of Christ from the height of the Cross.

—Fifteenth-century Welsh poet of Holywell, North Wales[2]

The centre of the world is thirteen feet to the west of Mount Calvary.

—Anonymous Christian writer, c. 1101–1104

I have written this book, for the love I bear towards you, about the Holy

Places. These are sanctified by the bodily presence of our Lord, the

Saviour of the world, and with him his glorious mother, Mary, Eternal

Virgin, and the blessed company of his Disciples.

—John of Wurzburg, c. 1170 [3]

One afternoon after a large group of half-naked, ash-coated yogis had passed by, singing and dancing and stopping the traffic for miles, B said quietly: "Do you know what this country does to you? It makes you believe against your will that at any moment the curtain of what you have called reality can part and reveal something amazing, fabulous."

—ANDREW HARVEY[4]

WHERE SHOULD YOU GO? TO WHERE THE BELOVED IS. BUT where is that? And why does the Beloved live there?

I have spent a lot of time in Jerusalem. Its fascination is endless and growing. When I am asked why I keep going back, the answer depends on the company. I might say that I can get about ten times as much done per hour in Jerusalem than anywhere else in the world; or that I get an exhilarating and comforting sense of context when I see the layers of the place piled crazily on top of each other; or that it's the place where you can best breathe the things that we normally only think; or, if I'm feeling sanctimonious, that God seemed to have a clear preference for the place, and it seems prudent to share it. All these things are true, but they are not the whole truth. They are elements of a bigger and more fundamental answer: even when you are standing at a bus stop in suburban Jerusalem, there is an unmistakable *knowledge* that you are just on one side of a very thin, leaky membrane separating this world from another. It is like being in C. S. Lewis's famous wardrobe. You can feel the fur coats on your cheek, and there are moments when you can almost feel a snowflake on your nose, or the brush of a pine tree. This is not because there is a chance that a brain-washed Palestinian teenager with a knapsack of semtex might be boarding the bus with you, ready to send you and everyone else to another world. I've been in far more dangerous places and have never had that sense of imminent encounter.

The early Christian Celts spoke about "thin places"—places where worlds (I would prefer to say "dimensions") were particularly close to each other. Places where, if you were quiet enough, you could hear the murmurings of God.

Archaeologists agree that, whatever human beings are, the things that make them quintessentially human are seen for the first time in the Upper Paleolithic. There is a vibrant and inconclusive debate about whether there was a sudden explosion of human consciousness in the Upper Paleolithic, or whether the apparent explosion in the archaeological record is an artifact, the truth being a gradual opening of distinctively human eyes. Whatever the truth, the distinctiveness of the new creature is dramatic. Go to a good museum. Look at the Upper Paleolithic shelves. You will see things that were not even foreshadowed in the periods before. There is an exuberant efflorescence of arts and music. The first men beat drums, danced to music, and represented themselves and the world around them in a colossal outpouring of symbol. The Upper Paleolithic revolution was a revolution marked most importantly by the ability to make mental models of the various possibilities in the universe, and a compulsion to make them.

Another thing happened then: religion. Some say that religion was a product of the symbolizing revolution; others say relationship to God catalyzed the obsessive symbolizing. But no serious scholars doubt that that is when it happened. Religion and symbol are intimately and fundamentally related at a historical and biological level, let alone a theological one. The relationship isn't a dusty abstraction. You can see it.

Near Aventignan, high in the French Pyrenees, are the Gargas caves. From 22,000–27,000 years ago, humans as neurologically modern as you are inhabited them. On the walls are nearly 250 handprints of adults and children made by placing the hand on the rock and blowing pigment around it, so that the outline of the hand is seen. Elsewhere in Europe, bison, elk, and other animals are beautifully and skillfully depicted but with some curious omissions. Some body parts seem to be missing. In fact they are not missing at all: the artists were indicating that they were on the other side of the rock. Those animals literally had one foot in another world. The Gargas hands were touching the membrane, represented by the rock wall that separated this world from the world of the spirits.[5] They were reaching out to the gods like charismatic hands in worship. For them, as for many others who came after, caves were the borders between the worlds. If you wanted to get close to those other worlds, you came there, to the thin places. You came on pilgrimage. These caves were votive places. The handprints weren't like wallpaper, decorating a place where you ate and slept.

In one of the famous Upper Paleolithic sites of southwest France, there is a sacred chamber. We know it is sacred because there is absolutely no point in going there for any other reason. It is absurdly inaccessible—an hour's crawl on hands and knees. Those early men crept often through the dark to get closer to whatever it was they thought was holy. They were pilgrims to thin places.

Jerusalem is the classic thin place. Whether God chose it because it was thin, or whether the membrane became thinner because it was pressed by the faithful feet or importunate hands of the pilgrims, I do not know. But I suspect both.

Prayer and maleficence can no doubt transform places. A place that has been prayed in is often warm and magnetic; a place that has been cursed or seen great evil shivers even in the sun. Birds do not sing in Auschwitz. But surely that is not all there is to a holy place. It doesn't explain God's ancient and emphatic preference for Jerusalem.

The notion of a holy place, a place where the divine is more than usually accessible, is ubiquitous and persistent. It started with caves, sacred groves, trees like the Norse Ydraggsill that linked the worlds and are now enshrined in stories like *Jack and the Beanstalk*, holy mountains and blessed springs; and moved on to churches, cities, and countries.

"Are there not many holy places on this earth?" asked the author of the "Kashi Khanda," one of the sections of the *Skanda Purana*, a Hindu holy book. And he continued:

> Yet which of them would equal in the balance one speck of Kashi's dust? Are there not many rivers running to the sea? Yet which of them is like the River of Heaven in Kashi? Are there not many fields of liberation on earth? Yet not one equals the smallest part of the city never forsaken by Shiva. The Ganges, Shiva and Kashi: Where this Trinity is watchful, no wonder here is found the grace that leads one on to perfect bliss.[6]

This sort of hymn is everywhere. "It demonstrates," said my friend Steve:

> a fundamental and corrosive misunderstanding of the relationship between God and humans. Christians must have nothing to do with these sorts of ideas. There is no such thing as a "holy place." All this talk about a veil separating this world from another exposes the fallacy very well. For when Jesus died, the veil separating the holy of holies from the outside world was torn down. The holy, previously penned in the Jerusalem temple, flooded out. There is now no distinction between the sacred and the secular. Everywhere is at least potentially holy.

> Whenever someone repents of his sins and turns to Jesus, a holy place is created in his heart. Jerusalem is no more holy than Heathrow Airport. You can meet with God equally easily in either place.

With the exception of two words, Steve was spot on. The words are "equally easily." Being the sort of creatures we are, places matter. We were not born simply into the world but to a specific place within it. The relationship between man and matter and man and place lends places a real and theologically legitimate significance. "Tell me the landscape in which you live," wrote Jose Ortega y Gasset, "and I will tell you who you are."[7] The Bible repeatedly tells us where people came from, as if those geographical origins told us something about the essence of the person: "Paul of Tarsus"; "Jesus of Nazareth"; "Simon of Cyrene"; "a man of Macedonia"; "Ruth the Moabite." Nomads are *from* places too.

William Golding spoke of the house in which he grew up as a repository of his "personal mythology," and places are commonly repositories of shared and crucial mythologies. Landscape changes people. Men are chameleons: if they lie close enough to the land, they look like it. That can be a good thing or a bad thing.

Pilgrimage is often spoken of as a return to one's own "sacred center." The words are guaranteed to raise modern Christian hackles and for good historical and not-so-good theological reasons. But it is difficult to avoid this sort of language in describing one's own experience of pilgrimage. The travelers' accounts often go along these lines:

> I went to the place to which I thought God was calling me—the place where he would do particular business with me. For me, that place was the center of the world. Indeed the center of the Universe, because he was there waiting for me with a smile. As I traveled closer to the place, and closer to him, I found that I was becoming more and more *myself*, more and more the person who I really was and was meant to be. All the peripheral stuff got stripped away. I was less and less anything other than that which was at the center of me. And I increasingly saw that what was at the center of me was made of the same stuff as him. He was the center of the holy city. As I approached the city, the "him in me," that was also Me, increasingly overlapped with him.

We need to be careful with accounts like this. Christianity repudiates the idea of an assimilation of people into God. As we approach God, we become more distinctively ourselves, not less. Nor does it say that everything in us is good and of God. God is holy, and there are many things in us that are not. But our proper caution should not deprive us of the splendid truths that many pilgrims discover. I challenge any reasonably sensitive pilgrim who has walked from Paris to Santiago to describe his experience in language that would not ring bells with an educated Hindu or Sufi. If you think that means the whole Santiago experience is satanic, I doubt you'll have read this far in this book, and we really have very little to say to one another.

The idea of a pilgrimage site as a place where God can be particularly intimately encountered is strong in Judaism and Christianity. And of course the place of places, the thinnest place of all, is Jerusalem. There are other chosen places, but Jerusalem is at the top of God's list. It is, very literally in many documents, the center. There is a sense that the other pilgrimage sites are subcenters—franchises, almost—permitted graciously to function because it is not always easy to get to Jerusalem. "Thus says the Lord GOD: This is Jerusalem; I have set her in the center of the nations, with countries all around her," Ezekiel 5:5 tells us. That was how Jewish and Christian traditions viewed her.

The Midrash Tanchuma, from the Roman era, teaches that

> as the navel is set in the centre of the human body, so is the land of Israel the navel of the world . . . situated in the centre of the world, and Jerusalem in the centre of the land of Israel, and the sanctuary in the centre of Jerusalem, and the holy place in the centre of the sanctuary, and the ark in the centre of the holy place, and the Foundation Stone before the holy place, because from it the world was founded. [8]

The crusaders agreed, except that by their time the exact center was not the foundation stone on the Temple Mount (now the *Sakhra*, the rock, holy to Islam, in the Dome of the Rock), but just around the corner: "[Jerusalem] is situated in the centre of the world, in the middle of the earth," wrote Jacques de Vitry, the Bishop of Acre, "so that all men may turn their steps towards her; she is the patrimony of the patriarchs, the nurse of the prophets, the mistress of the apostles, the cradle of our salvation, the home of our Lord, and the mother of our Faith."[9] That was long the orthodoxy. The fifteenth-century traveler William Wey laboriously copied out into his pocket book a Greek inscription from a mortise stone in the Church of the Holy Sepulchre: "Here God wrought salvation in the centre of the earth."[10]

If you go to Hereford Cathedral in England, you can see the famous Mappa Mundi (map of the world), dated to about 1300. Jerusalem is at the very center—the point around which all other geography revolves, as all theology revolves. Modern guides in the Church of the Holy Sepulchre in Jerusalem will point out, in a matter-of-fact way, the *omphalos*—the navel of the world—just east of the tomb of Christ. The perceived connection between the physical Jerusalem and the spiritual realms was so intimate that some confused and conflated them. Some of the simpler foot soldiers on the People's Crusade really thought they were marching to the New Jerusalem, a mistake their leaders took no pains to correct. We see the same thinking in some naive brands of modern Christian Zionism.

Jewish thinkers have generally understood the legitimate Christian apocalyptic tradition rather better than most of the Christians. "According to our teachers," says the *Zohar*, the most important of the kabbalistic writings, "God fashioned the lower Jerusalem on the model of the heavenly Jerusalem, the one exactly facing the other. God will in time cause the upper Jerusalem to descend below . . . the Mother [will] join the Daughter and the two [will] become one."[11]

It's not surprising that people want to go to Jerusalem. It's not just where it all happened; it's where it is all going to happen.

"We're not on this planet long," said Klaus, a German pilgrim to Jerusalem, over the boiled eggs at the Lutheran Guesthouse. "And so I don't want to mess around on the margins of things. I want authenticity. I want to be at the center. Why should I go to a Christian theme park when I can come to Jerusalem? Why should I read the newspapers when I can read Shakespeare?"

Yes, insist on going to the center, but don't make the mistake that the Mappa Mundi and Klaus made. Steve was more right than we originally gave him credit for being. The death and resurrection of Jesus did result in a massive reshaping of the spiritual geography of the universe. There has been a decentralization of the fountainhead of grace. Jerusalem, in Israel/Palestine, has conclusively and importantly lost its monopoly.

Let's be clear about what this means and what it doesn't mean. The first point is the one Steve made: Heathrow is a holy place. But as we've seen already, some people resonate more with some places than others. Many, including me, have found for whatever reason that it is helpful to be in Jerusalem. Is that theology? I don't know; I have no idea where theology ends and Carl Jung, Rupert Sheldrake, or other would-be explainers of the connection between people and places begin. The more fundamental point, though, is that the God who is Jesus is a God whose nature is always and inevitably expressed in paradox. If you try to be the greatest, you will be the least. If you go headlong for the center, ignoring the journey there and the marginal lands you go through on the way, you will certainly miss the center. In the Christian pilgrimage tradition, uniquely, the arrival point is less important than the journey. It is not quite true to say that the arrival is irrelevant (and certainly our eternal destination is important), but although the intention is to meet with a saint at shrine X, you'll find that you will meet with him, and greater than him, in the slums outside the city. The meetings you thought would happen in the throne room in the center of a royal palace actually happen in a urine-drenched bus shelter. And that's because the bus shelter is the palace.

"Where your treasure is, there your heart will be also," said Jesus,[12] from which it follows that where your heart is, your treasure will be found. Where should you go? It sounds corny, but you should follow your heart. If, as you sit at your desk, your heart is telling you about huge, gray skies; crashing breakers; and whirling gulls, perhaps you should be going to Iona. If you wake with dreams of hot rock, icy stars, and a silence so deep you can hear the blood move in your toes, maybe you need to go and sit in a desert. If you have heard the ancient *Gayatri* mantra sung in Sanskrit and known that the universe stands still to hear it, perhaps you need to sit cross-legged in the dark at Bede Griffiths' Shantivanam Ashram in Tamil Nadu as the bats flicker around the palms and the Benedictine monks chant it as part of the Eucharist:

Om bhur bhura svata
Tat savitur varenyam
Bhargo devasaya dhimahi
Dhigo yo nah prachchodyat

That translates, "Salutations to the Word, which is present in the earth, the sky and that which is beyond. Let us meditate on the glorious splendor of that divine Giver of Life. May he illuminate our meditation." Warn yourself about pantheism, if you're feeling insecure, but the monks don't have horns, truly. If you have the courage and the faith (and I don't), perhaps you should set yourself adrift in an open boat like those Irish monks, trusting to the hand that fans the wind.

Above all, do not let anyone, least of all the writer of a book on pilgrimage, tell you where to go. It is nothing to do with anyone else.

But wherever you go, go.

8

PACKING AND PREPARATION

Simplicity. Simplicity. Simplicity. I say, let your affairs be as two or three, and not a hundred or a thousand; instead of a million count half a dozen, and keep your accounts on your thumbnail.

—HENRY DAVID THOREAU[1]

Hasten quickly to Jerusalem, and make no delay.

—WILLIAM WEY[2]

THIS IS A SHORT CHAPTER. I DON'T WANT TO MAKE IT ANY longer because that might suggest that leaving is harder than it is. The summary: go. Don't take much. Don't worry too much about preparing. The journey itself will prepare you for whatever you need to be prepared for.

Lao Tzu, twenty-five hundred years ago, pointed out something that is easily forgotten: "A journey of a thousand miles begins with a single step."[3] "Whatever you can do, or dream you can, begin it," urged one explorer. "Boldness has genius, power, and magic in it."[4] If leaving now would mean you went without your most comfortable boots, go without your most comfortable boots. You'll be given a new sort of comfort. Let the journey model the sort of reckless Jesus-following Christianity *is*. Those fishermen left their livelihoods *immediately* and started to follow. If, while being considerate to others, you can go now, go now.

What should you take? Far less than you think you need. Let the road supply it. Take Matthew 10:9–10 as literally as you can: "Take no gold, or silver, or copper in your belts, no bag for your journey, or two tunics, or sandals, or a staff."[5] It's a slightly different world now. But you don't need more than one shirt: the one you have will wash. The bag you planned to take is far too big. What you will need will depend on where you're going, but you shouldn't need much more than your passport, a credit card, some small denomination bills, a sweater, one spare set of socks and underclothes, and a lightweight waterproof jacket. Whether you take books will depend on whether there will be other people there. If there will be, make *them* your books. Out of neurotic habit, I always take Robert Fagles's translation of *The Odyssey*. I also take a small, stained, zip-up Bible, but I can't pretend that I read it much on the road.

When you have collected the things you plan to take, ask of each of them, "Is that there to insulate me from what the journey has in store?" If it is, leave it behind. (*The Odyssey* certainly falls into that class; I'm a hypocrite.) To a terrifying extent, we are simply lists of the things we have. Our dependence on them is so complete that we have come to have no existence apart from them. A really small bag can help to give us back ourselves.

Read, and largely ignore, the packing lists that have come down to us from medieval pilgrims. You should have a barrel for wet and dry supplies, advised William Wey. "Make sure you have a lantern and candles, bedding, and cooking utensils, and even a chamber pot in case you are too sick to go up on deck to use the normal facilities."[6] There is a chandler in Venice, just before St. Mark's, he tells us, who will give you a feather bed, pillow, and sheets on a sale or return basis. Wey sought and obtained from Pope Pius a special indulgence to take along a portable altar. In his traveler's guide to the Holy Land, he provides an early phrase book, which lets us ask the locals, "Where is the tavern?" and "Woman, have ye good wine?"—interests he shared with Merry Andrew, who prescribed wine for pilgrims on a medicinal pretext (it "doth quicken a man's wit, comfort his heart, and scour his liver") and who urged, "You must bye a bygge cheste with a locke and kaye to kepe-in wyne . . . and other necessary things."[7] Santo Brasca of Milan, who traveled to the Holy Land in 1480, had a list strikingly similar to Wey's. He thought that a night stool or a covered pail were essential (for obvious reasons), as were a barrel of wine and a barrel of water, an overcoat reaching to the ground (for sleeping out—a very practical and economical idea, from which we could well learn), syrup of ginger to settle the stomach, and a copious supply of fruit syrup (good for the heat, he thought). Along similar lines, it might not be breaching the rule of simplicity too badly to put some antidiarrheals and some rehydration sachets in that small pack of yours.

By all means, when you have decided where you are going, consult with others about the effect of your absence, and about the practicalities of the journey. A pilgrimage is not a selfish jaunt. It does not entitle you to say that God has commanded you to wash your hands of all responsibilities. Don't leave others to mop up the mess that you have left. That's not pilgrimage; that's exploitation. Clear your in-tray, leave everything in order, and set an away message on your e-mail.

When Irish St. Brendan heard from a visiting monk, Barrind, about a mysterious island in the west called the Promised Land, Brendan was desperate to go. But he was part of a community and couldn't just drop his tools. He called his monks together and put the issue to them: "From you who are dear to me, and share the good fights with me, I look for advice and help, for my heart and all my thoughts are fixed on one determination . . . to go in search of the Promised Land of the Saints."[8]

Consider a ceremony to bless, or at least mark, the start of the pilgrimage. It shouldn't be complicated, and it shouldn't delay your departure. But it will mark you out in your own eyes and the eyes of others as someone with a new commission. You'll be embarrassed to cancel your plans after such a ceremony, and that embarrassment is thoroughly good. It will be a more or less irrevocable first step, and a first step that is explicitly blessed is more likely to be followed by other blessed steps. Habits are important: get into the habit of holiness.

The Muslim writer Amir Soltai Sheikholeslami writes about ceremonies of departure in his native Iran:

> Growing up in Iran, it was impossible to set out on a journey without having my grandmother rush behind us with the family Quran in hand, make us step back into the house, and then circle the Quran above our heads while calling on the Prophet Mohammed and his household to safeguard our travel. Sacred scripture . . . would be puffed around us like a divine fragrance. We would kiss the holy book, and only then could my brother and I step out of the door.[9]

That grandmother knew the votive power of journeys. She knew that to send travelers out with their feet wading through the "divine fragrance" of prayer was to turn each step into a prayer, just as each flap of a Buddhist prayer flag or each turn of a prayer wheel can be. Her prayers contrast sharply with the mumbled, halfhearted requests for "traveling mercies" we often hear in Christian churches.

We've looked already at the purification ceremonies and some of the rituals of abstinence and simplicity used by some travelers. Consider them. Don't be enslaved by them. But they might be useful. If the road is indeed a holy place, and you aim to get holier on it, then start now. Perhaps mark your departure by a physical ritual of purification. It need not be formal. Swim across a river. Take a cold bath. Burn all your clothes except the ones in which you'll walk, and cook sausages on the bonfire.

There is an ambitious Chinese Zen Song of Pilgrimage, cited by Thomas Merton, which sets out the cry of an ideal pilgrim. Aspire to it, but don't beat yourself up when you fail:

> His conduct is to be transparent as ice or crystal.
>
> He is not to seek fame or wealth.
>
> He is to rid himself of defilements of all sorts.
>
> He has no other way open to him but to go about and inquire.
>
> Let him be trained in mind and body by walking over the mountains and fording the rivers.
>
> Let him befriend wise men in the Dharma [Law] and pay them respect whenever he may accost them.
>
> Let him brave the snow, tread on the frosty roads, not minding the severity of the weather.
>
> Let him cross the waves and penetrate the clouds, chasing away dragons and evil spirits.[10]

Of course there are some Christian caveats. The purpose is not primarily to "inquire," but to meet: the "wise men" are all the people you bump into, particularly if they're on heroin and state benefits. Don't go looking for dragons or evil spirits; they'll come looking for you and will run screaming when they see you.

9

THE JOURNEY: OLD FEET, NEW EYES

Enthusiasm normally manifests itself with all of its force during the first years of our lives. At that time, we still have strong links with the divinity, and we throw ourselves into our play with our toys with such a will that dolls take on life and our tin soldiers actually march.

—Paulo Coelho[1]

A good traveller does not, I think, much mind the uninteresting places. He is there to be inside them, as a thread is inside the necklace it strings. The world, with unknown and unexpected variety, is a part of his own leisure; and this participation is, I think, what separates the traveller and the tourist, who remains separate, as if he were at a theatre, and not himself a part of whatever the show may be.

—Freya Stark[2]

I walked only at night. Not, as the desert Arabs do, because it was hot. This was Scotland. But nasty things had happened in the day, and the night was kinder, and I wanted to urge my senses awake again. We don't need eyes, ears, or noses like the ones we have during the urban day. They are bombarded by impulses hugely heavier than the ones they are designed for, and they lose their sensitivity. I wanted to need them again, to see what they could do, to see what there was out there that I was missing, and to be the sort of animal I was designed to be.

During the day I slept in the heather, in groves of dwarf oak, and on the sea-loch side. I had a waterproof sleeping bag but tried not to use it. The sun burned the dew from my clothes within a couple of hours of sunrise, and I wanted to wear that haze as the land does. I had a growing fear of meeting anyone, and I was proud of that fear. It showed that I was making progress. With the fear came acuity. I could see the deer across the far side of the glen, hear the otter splash before it whistled, and smell the stale men who had gathered sheep an hour before. I surprised a fox. I wrote adolescent things in a notebook. I took off my boots because their noise was an abomination and because they stopped me from feeling where I was and how vulnerable I really was. I envied the Hindu *sannyasis*, who wander India "sky-clothed" (stark naked), and I reflected on how much more intensely than I they live and how much more literally in the minimalistic spirit of travel Jesus had urged. And then I laughed for envying someone for having absolutely nothing and thought that I ought to do this more, and that if I did, I might become a proper person.

And then I got tired and bored and caught a train back to London.

"Man," wrote Albert Camus, "is the only creature who refuses to be what he is."[3]

Every pilgrimage is a journey backward. Every pilgrim's step is a step toward his childhood. And that, in the paradoxical logic of the kingdom, is the only way to go forward. It is only children who inherit the kingdom.

There's little that is new in most of our days. That, perversely, is how we like it. We arrange our lives to avoid the terror of novelty, fencing it out with routine, with insurance, with the company of people who agree with us. But for the young child, everything is new. She has never seen a postman before, and his uniform is dazzlingly romantic. When she looks at a cat, she sees teeth, hair, and danger—in fact, origins and essence—in a way we never do. When she looks at a concrete wasteland, it is populated with monsters and fascinations.

The pilgrim can be the same, although it takes time and the practice of vulnerability. He has many advantages over the stay-at-home. He's on a peninsula of the kingdom where the rules are different—where the first is last, the greatest is least, and the child is the sage. He will know something of the freedom that those rules give him, and that knowledge will help him to overcome his fear of abandoning his expensive, ridiculous, ill-fitting adulthood. If he has companions, they will laugh at him when he talks like a secretary of state, and that will help too.

Every step he takes along an unfamiliar road gives him, as the whole world gives the child, a completely new view. The journey is a string of thrilling unfamiliarities, and therefore a string of vehicles back to the nursery. If he chooses wisely and avoids taking his cultural comforts with him in the form of people from his own church or town, he won't understand the language in which most things are said, just like a young child, and he will find that there are other, more intimate and articulate ways of understanding. If he is sensible enough not to book ahead and has no way of knowing where he will next eat, or whether he will, or where he will sleep, his relationship to the environment will be transformed. He'll be catapulted back to the dependency he knew when he was screaming on his mother's knee and relied entirely on something other than himself for very life. If you are placentally plugged into the land, receiving everything from it, you will never fail to remark to yourself on its character. Not noticing isn't an option.

Actually, of course, our dependency is always complete. Most of what we call our "lives" is composed of elaborate devices designed to let us perpetuate the absurd delusion of self-reliance. But you can't put many in your backpack. If your backpack is small enough, you can't fit any. The pilgrim moves through time at the pace of the pace, the pace time itself travels. He can't go much faster or much slower than his average. If a town is thirty miles away, he's not going to be there for dinner in two hours. Time and geography conspire against him and can't be frustrated.

He meets both head-on, probably (if he's from a Western culture) for the first time since infancy. The child, too, has a real relationship with time, undistorted by the accelerating effect of deadlines and airplanes, the decelerating effect of boredom, or the artificial punctuation of alarms.

The pilgrim's prayer, to be spoken as a mantra in time to each step, is, "Make me a child; make me a child; make me a child." The prayer is necessary. The intention and the road will go a long way toward making it happen, but there is always a shortfall. You need new eyes. That demands an act of creation, not just rehabilitation. The sort of new eyes God gives aren't just, or even mainly, designed for seeing the buds you would previously have missed or the nuances of your relationship with a particular pile of rocks. They are designed to let you see Jesus in the world, and we're given some pretty emphatic clues about where to look.

If you're Christian and you have lost your first Love, a pilgrimage can help you to fall in love again, only better and more fully, for the best is always yet to be. It can give you the ability to love as a child loves—a love without cynicism, suspicion, or envy.

"A man's work is nothing but this slow trek to rediscover, through the detours of art, those two or three great and simple images in whose presence his heart first opened," wrote Camus.[4] He was writing about the artistic life, and I think he was right. But the statement holds true of life more generally. Substitute *life* for *work* and delete "through the detours of art," and you've something very profound. Pilgrimage can be the literal slow trek that gives sight of those heart-opening images. And it can also forge and explain the connection between those formative aboriginal images and the God we worship. It can teach us that at the base of our being, at the heart of everything we really love and value, God is. And was. It can help us to know that when we first opened our eyes in wonder at this dazzling, kaleidoscopic world and were cocooned in unconditional love, God was the source of the color and the love. It's a very fundamental sort of redemption—a sort of retrospective infant baptism. It baptizes our childhood and heals the shattered connection between childhood and adulthood. It's a kind of rebirth.

But there are dangers. Since we are not used to newness, it can be terrifying. We can find ourselves crying out for the old, drab certainties. Our fear can harden us. Some people react by clinging ever more tightly to the nine-to-five persona. The crust that grows from a lifetime of being steeped in littleness, routine, sycophancy, and egotism can thicken, rather than being rubbed off. There will always be a few people whose inability to cope with the rigors of the road sends them back home as fastidious, whining bigots, complaining about the food, the hardness of the beds, and the "dreadful, smelly, snoring people, who couldn't even speak proper English, but did insist on talking to me all the time." Those people are in a very dangerous position. Pilgrimage, one of the most potent cures for chronic unreality ever devised, has failed. Pilgrimage always changes the pilgrim: sometimes it makes him worse, not better.

Life and journeying are a lot more fun with those reborn eyes. Not only will you see the hare, but also you will begin to see *why* the hare. Next you will see that one of the purposes of your being called out of nonexistence was to see the hare, and that one of the purposes of it being squeezed out of its mother was to see you. With every neonatal blink, you will see new connections between you and the landscape, and you will feel progressively less alone. You will rejoice that the wet asphalt of the road sparkles as it does. You will increasingly be able to attribute joy to Joy himself. You will change the landscape as it changes you. You are inside it, and it cannot help being changed. Hindu pilgrims made a sacred landscape of India, and you will know what they mean. You will feel your effect on the landscape as an ecstatic partnership, not an onerous responsibility. You will struggle not to use pantheistic language, but you'll never have been less of a pantheist in your life.

"When you are moving towards an objective," says Petrus, Paulo Coelho's guide on the road to Santiago de Compostela, "it is very important to pay attention to the road. It is the road that teaches us the best way to get there, and the road enriches us as we walk its length."[5] That's true, and although our heightened and heightening senses will be crying out for more and more data to process, it is a necessary caution. In my Zen days, on other sorts of journeys, cross-legged in the ice-cold meditation hall, watching my breathing going in and out, hovering around my breaths, the screech of the master would cut into the night and into the fuzzy shadow lands around the core of my concentration: "Pay attention." It was always timely. Now I know there are better things to watch than breaths. Or at least *other* things.

One thing that all this will do is make you more and more conscious of metaphor. As you see your place in things, you will learn effortlessly the lessons that the road has to teach, many of them taught in the language of metaphor. It is yet another of those ironies in which the kingdom delights: as you become more literal, more stripped to the core, you become increasingly sensitive to symbolism. You become much closer to the Upper Paleolithic prototype. And if anyone wants to build an Adamic theology on that, they're welcome. It would be completely coherent.

Since the lessons are so obvious and so inevitable, I can see no point in spelling them out here. Yes, at the start of the day you had no idea what the day would bring, would not have started if you had, but are glad you went on anyway. Yes, you get a better view from high hills. Yes, there is a rainbow after the storm. Yes, all those observations can be used, perfectly properly, to season sermons. I'm not at all mocking the illustrations or saying they are illegitimate. I'm just saying you don't need me to highlight them. But there is one thing I need to say. It is so obvious that it is easily missed.

You are on the road for a lot longer, usually, than you are at the destination. It is there the real work is often done. That's one of the reasons, I suggest, why *Christian* pilgrimage, with its historic emphasis on the journey rather than the arrival, is particularly devotionally useful. The metaphors from the journey are directly applicable to the everyday business of living. Back at home we spend all our time traveling from birth to death; arrival isn't something we know much about. You can lift the lessons from the road to the office; it is harder (although I'll try) to lift the lessons of arrival.

If arrival isn't the whole point, and the whole pilgrimage is metaphorically significant, what is the significance of the places where the journey is spent? The whole journey is spent in the hinterland of the sacred objective. Most of the learning is done, and most of the encounters occur on the *margins*; in the *outskirts*; in the dowdy, forgotten provinces. And that, in Scripture and in life, is where our hippie, non-mainstream, iconoclastic God is to be found. Don't look for him in constitutions or palaces; he loathes them. Look for him at the edge of the town, at the end of the day, at the center of a party so off-center that your mother would be appalled.

I've sometimes talked as if it is all grind, as if the joys are as pedestrian as the pedestrian. It is not so. There are sometimes moments of epiphany when your arms have to stretch ecstatically in worship. That, too, is like life, but the moments come more easily on the trail. Your arms are lighter because you're not carrying so much, and they lift more easily. Your sense of smell is better. You can sniff incense from miles away.

Sometimes you can hear God rolling toward you on the road. You wait, braced, for him to crash over you. Sometimes, almost at the edge of vision, you see the Spirit beginning to stalk you, and you know that sometime soon you will be consumed; you will know that you are unconditionally adored, accepted, and utterly safe. Tears will come.

Habitual tourists may be reading this and feeling left out. Good. Sorry, but what you do isn't what we're talking about here. A religious tourist in the holy sites of Rome or Santiago is an invulnerable pilgrim. An invulnerable pilgrim is an oxymoronic creature, like a four-legged biped. Certainly pilgrims can read guidebooks, see the sights, and tick boxes on clipboards; but tourists can't get new eyes while remaining tourists. Curiosity is fine. How wrong was that covert Gnostic Augustine to denounce pilgrims' curiosity as a "worthless stock . . . an interruption or distraction from our prayers."[6] But Thomas à Kempis, although he shared Augustine's life-denying disapproval of curiosity, was right to observe that "one seldom hears that any amendment of life results [from mere sightseeing]."[7] Grace is great and can do wonders even in St. Peter's Square in August, but eye-renewing grace finds it difficult to get into an air-conditioned bus. Being physical animals, what happens to our bodies affects what happens to our minds and souls.

10

THE JOURNEY:
BLISTERED FEET, TIRED EYES

Mine is a generation that circles the globe and searches for something
we haven't tried before. So never refuse an invitation, never resist
the unfamiliar, never fail to be polite, and never outstay the
welcome. Just keep your mind open and suck in the experience.
And if it hurts, you know what? It's probably worth it.

—ALEX GARLAND[1]

A LITTLE WHILE AGO I SKIED TO THE NORTH POLE, FOR NO
good reason. I was fitter then and started off fast and arrogantly. That meant I had to stop and wait for the others, who
were more intelligent, to catch up. It meant I got cold.

At the end of the first day on the ice, I took off my glove.
The tip of my third finger on my left hand (a hand already
badly injured in a rock-climbing accident, and vulnerable to the
cold) was white and rock hard. It was frozen solid, like meat in a
freezer, which is exactly what it was. Being selfish, and not both-
ering too much about the worry of the others, I didn't mind

much. I knew I would lose the end of the finger, but you really don't need ten fingers.

A few months later, on a blistering summer day in England, I was playing with the black, necrotic tip, when the distal phalanx snapped off in my hand. I went to the local hospital, wearing shorts and a T-shirt, and asked them if they could trim my frostbitten finger for me. The nurse looked at me as if I needed an urgent psychiatric referral, which people continue to suggest.

I now have the fingertip in a plastic box in my desk drawer. I sometimes take it to lectures and rattle it if people look bored.

That was an example of an injury suffered in the course of a pilgrimage—in that case a pilgrimage to the shrine of my own ego, a shrine at which I am a devout, disciplined, and regular worshipper.

Other pilgrims have suffered much greater hardships in the pursuit of greater goals. Saewulf wrote of his journey in 1102:

We climbed up from Joppa [Jaffa] to the city of Jerusalem, a journey of two days, along a mountainous road, rocky, and very dangerous. For the Saracens, always laying snares for the Christians, lie hidden in the hollow places of the mountains, and the caves of the rocks, watching day and night, and always on the lookout for those whom they can attack . . . Oh, what a number of human bodies, both in the road and by the side of it, lie all torn by wild beasts.[2]

Bunyan, although he was writing allegorically, compiled an impressive catalog of the real dangers facing pilgrims. Kidnapping and robbing were common hazards for medieval and not-so-medieval pilgrims. In Bunyan, Giant Despair towers over the pilgrims, demanding, menacingly, why they are "trampling and lying on my grounds." They are taken off to Doubting Castle, where they are flung into a dungeon; deprived of water, food, and light; beaten with a "grievous crab-tree Cudgel;" and told that the best way out is suicide. Christian escaped, of course.[3] Many others were not so lucky. When the authorities opened the backyard shed of a medieval French boardinghouse owner, they found the corpses of eighty-eight pilgrims stacked neatly like sacks of rice.[4] It was commonplace to be harried by Turkish pirates on the way from Venice to Jaffa, to be forced on pain of death to buy extortionately priced bogus relics on the road back to London from Canterbury, and to have to pay vast bribes to the Saracens, who governed the Holy Land for much of the Middle Ages. The woodlands that covered Europe in the heyday of pilgrimage were the rustling, hooting, haunted home of robber bands. Night in the woods was no friend.

Navigation was another problem highlighted by Bunyan, and it is still easily possible, when your GPS batteries fail, to lose your way on some of the remoter tributaries of the Camino to Santiago, on the moors en route to the holy island of Lindisfarne, in the terraced highlands and gray plains of central America as you search for the votive places of the Mayas, as you search for

Himalayan stupas that hold yeti scalps, or in the hot, scented streets of India, where the air is thick with antiquity and confusion. "O that I had kept my way!" whines Bunyan's Hopeful.[5] "Consult your map constantly," Bunyan wants you to conclude. "It's called the Bible."

Bunyan spends a lot of time warning against the dangers of vice. The pilgrim, if he is to stand any chance of reaching the Holy City, must resist the blandishments of Vanity Fair, the embodiment of worldly superficiality. If he spends his money on the fripperies on sale there—the "Places, Honours, Preferments, Titles, Lusts, Pleasures and Delights of all sorts . . . Whores, Bawds . . . Silver, Gold, Precious Stones, Pearls, and what not," he will have nothing left to carry him further along the road. It has other dangers: "Thefts, Murders, Adulteries, False Swearers"—as Christian and Faithful, falsely accused of slander, discover. Christian escapes with his life: Faithful is burnt at the stake as so many Protestants had been by Catholics, and so many Catholics had been by Protestants.[6]

Bunyan's allegory falters at Vanity Fair. Most people are only on the road because they have managed to put Vanity Fair behind them. The relief of doing so is usually so intense that there is no desire to go back. There are no bosses to suck up to on the road, no appraisals other than the ones that you and God give to yourself; you have given up climbing the greasy pole so that you can climb the final rise that will give you the view of the golden dome and the Judean desert echoing beyond it; and you're probably too tired to want to jump into bed with the willowy, sun-tanned German temptress who walked beside you for a few miles. Not that you could, anyway, for adultery is tricky when you're sharing a dormitory with twenty others. Yes, there are shady characters and threats. I've been beaten up and deported from Delhi, and hunted in Kathmandu by a corrupt policeman in search of a payoff; but unless you have a kilo of cocaine in your luggage (yet another reason for a small bag), these are colorful annoyances, good for the retelling, rather than real challenges.

Then there are natural hazards, exemplified by Bunyan's famous Slough of Despond, "the low ground where the scum and filth of a guilty conscience, caused by conviction of sin, continually gather."[7] Medieval pilgrims feared low places, too, because they hummed with malaria-carrying mosquitoes, but more fearsome were the towns, where the Black Death lurked, and the high, cold places. The notorious St. Bernard Pass, used by many pilgrims to cross the Alps toward Rome, claimed many lives. Aelfrige, Archbishop of Canterbury, froze to death there in 959; in 1188, John of Canterbury's beard "congealed in a long icicle," and his inkbottle froze solid.[8]

But it is the discomforts, rather than the dangers, that fill the nighttime conversations in the pilgrim hostels. Nothing changes. Modern travelers moan about food, drink, sleeping conditions, toilet facilities, and general squalor. And so did their forebears: "The falafel tastes of zinc, and because the fridge had packed up, the fish was green," said Andy in Jerusalem in 2009. The bread is full of worms, and the wine is "hot and tasteless," noted Hans von Mergenthal, on his way to the Holy Land in 1476.[9] *Retsina is disgusting*, thought Canon Pietro Casola, en route to Jerusalem in 1494: "It leaves a very strange odour which does not please me."[10] "How can the Greeks drink that stuff?" spat Catharine, a modern maenad, walking from Athens to Delphi in 2007. "The sleeping space allotted to each pilgrim was so narrow that the passengers almost lay one on the other, tormented by the great heat, by swarms of insects, and even by great rats that raced over their bodies in the dark," wrote von Mergenthal.[11] "Leg room on the plane was appalling," said Cody. "I got no more than a couple of hours' sleep, a child was crying a couple of rows back, the choice of in-flight movies was dismal, and cabin service left a lot to be desired."

The "places necessary for purging the body" stuck out from the side of the Venetian galley, hanging precariously over the sea, Pietro Casola carefully tells us, noting with relief that the seat seems to be of "timber well tarred and joined together."[12] The perils of the bathroom continue on land. The Cretans "all empty the vessels from the windows without taking any precautions . . . though the contents should fall on a person's head, no penalty is incurred . . . there is a great stink."[13] The toilet obsession is the same in every age: "Do you know," said Anne, "the bathrooms were unbelievable. In one place there was no seat at all. I had to call reception and get them to move me to another room." Arculf, writing about his visit to Jerusalem about AD 670, prissily notes that "the very great number of . . . camels and horses and asses, not to speak of the mules and oxen . . . strews the streets of the city here and there with the abomination of their excrements, the smell of which brings no ordinary nuisance to the citizens and even makes walking difficult."[14]

None of the modern whinings I have quoted came from a real pilgrim. (Andy, Catherine, Cody, and Anne were tourists.) That's because I couldn't find any example from a pilgrim. And that's significant. A pilgrimage is transmuted into a package tour by the first sound of a whine. There are three possible pilgrim attitudes to hardship. One is to find that the hardships are not hardships at all. The bread that you'd have thrown away at home becomes a feast in the roadside field. The sleeping bag on the sand is actually more comfortable, and a lot better for your back, than the spongy mattress you left behind in your oppressively centrally heated bedroom. Another is to put up cheerfully with the hardships: to laugh at the rain; to know that the blister won't be so bad tomorrow, and anyway someone else has ruptured his Achilles, and so who are you to complain? The third is positively to rejoice in your sufferings.

Paul, of course, was keen on this.[15] I'm not at all sure I've understood him properly. Yes, I realize that there is an arguable difference between rejoicing in something and enjoying it. But if he means what he seems to mean, I find it difficult to follow him and put my inability down to the undoubted fact that he was a Christian mega-hero, and I am not. I can only say that all

the people I have ever met who have actively enjoyed their sufferings have been deviants. The Middle Ages were full of them.
Remember that splendid scene in *Monty Python and the Holy Grail*
where monks shuffle around a village, chanting in Latin, and
then hitting themselves on the head with the wooden boards
they were carrying? There were real people like that. They
were called the Flagellants, and they were no fun at all. They
went on perpetual pilgrimage throughout Europe, marching in
austere columns, two abreast; thrashing themselves with whips
to atone for the sins they thought had brought the Black Death,
and droning, miserably,

> *Ye murderers and ye robbers all,*
> *The wrath of God on you shall fall.*
> *Had it not been for our contrition,*
> *All Christendom had met perdition.*[16]

There are still plenty of people like that. They need to do an
Alpha course.

Jesus said you should take only one shirt for the journey. If
he'd meant a hair shirt, he'd have said so. There's no room in
that little bag for a second, penitential one. There will be hardships enough. Don't go looking for them.

For me, the greatest hardship of all is simply the time
these trips take. I get desperately homesick. I miss my wife, my
children, my college dinners, and the way the sun plays in the

courtyard of the Bodleian Library in Oxford. I beat myself up for being an irresponsible, absentee father and husband. But I have generally found there is a reason for the time things take.

After seven years of traveling, St. Brendan reached the Promised Land at the end of the world. There he met a youth who explained to him why it took so long. "You could not find it immediately because God wanted to show you his varied secrets in the great ocean."[17] When I plan to come back on the tenth day, and the plans are agonizingly frustrated, the great things happen on the eleventh. "How long the road is," mused Dag Hammarskjold. "But, for all the time the journey has already taken, how you have needed every second of it in order to learn what the road passes by."[18]

For most modern pilgrims, though, the real dangers are inherent in the really valuable lessons. If you go alone, there are terrible psychological hazards. The memory of them makes me shudder and run into a crowded bar. But most pilgrimages are jolly, sociable times. That does not make them safe.

We have looked already at the dangers of novelty. There is another danger, closely related to it. Human beings seem to be terrified of linearity—moving in a straight line. Time moves in a straight line. So does history, and so, if the Christians are right, does theology. But although (or perhaps because) we were dumped straight from our mothers' wombs onto a straight conveyor belt called history, we are rarely at home with time, and in particular with its unnerving straightness. We try to escape from it using lots of ingenious devices. We are comforted by the cycle of the seasons, and we love recurring festivals. Once we get to a certain age, we like most the festivals that simply mark the season, rather than those intimidating birthdays—the staging posts that remind us of our march along that dead-straight road to death. We make our own pathetic little festivals to convince ourselves that we're really in a cycling universe: tea with Sue every Monday; a drink with John every Wednesday; the Thursday morning board meeting; the immovable Saturday afternoon golf. The circular schemes of Eastern religion are hugely attractive to many, along with the warm, globular feel of the language that describes them. We instinctively prefer the idea of reincarnation to the icy Christian notion that "man lives once, and then comes judgment"[19] Usually the stern rules of cause and effect can be frustrated or their rigor mitigated. If you don't do that report, someone else eventually will. If you miss the bus, another will be along in ten minutes.

The road laughs at all our evasions. There are no festivals. Time plods. You have to cope with relentless newness. The world is new every step, let alone every morning. Cause and effect cannot be escaped or forgotten. If you walk, you will get there. If you don't, you won't. That's the way the world is designed. The road rubs our noses in reality, and it can be very painful and frightening.

The road interrogates us. That can be discomforting. People sweat in the witness box. What does the road think it is? The questions come faster and faster. They cannot be avoided forever. There's no lunch with your friends around the corner to give you an excuse for not answering them. No, you're not too busy to deal with such important things, which is the excuse you always give when you're at work. You have nothing to do today, or the day after that, or the week after that but to walk along this road. The road demands answers: What do you believe? Who are you? How did you become that person? Are you going to be this way forever? Would it matter if you died tonight?

Usually the response to this sort of questioning is a growing, fecund humility. It is one of the most attractive of human characteristics, which is why people who have traveled a lot make the best lovers. Sometimes that humility gets warped. It becomes self-hatred, for which the only medicine is love (which can work dramatically). Those self-hating travelers (I used to be one) turn part of their hatred outward. It becomes the world-weary travelers' cynicism, which you can hear in any backpacker's hostel, and it's so boring to listen to. But I suspect that it's not such a dangerous condition. It indicates that the traveler longs for more than the journey can give. You can go straight from that longing to the epistle to the Romans.

There is no need to be afraid. In fact there is every reason not to be. The valley of the shadow of death is part of Jerusalem, the city of redemption. The dark pilgrimage road is part of the kingdom, and the King himself, inveterate walker that he is, is usually at your side. There may be times in life when he is not. The great mystics have spoken of it as "the dark night of the soul." "The silence and the emptiness [in my heart are] so great that I look and do not see, listen and do not hear," Mother Teresa told a spiritual adviser. In a note written in 1955, she said, "The more I want Him, the less I am wanted . . . Such deep longing for God—and . . . repulsed—empty—no faith—no love—no zeal."[20] She also wrote a letter to Jesus:

> Lord, my God, who am I that You should forsake me? The child of your love—and now become as the most hated one . . . You have thrown away as unwanted—unloved . . . So many unanswered questions live within me . . . [I am] afraid to uncover them—because of the blasphemy—If there be a God—please forgive me . . . I am told that God loves me, and yet the reality of darkness and coldness and emptiness is so great that nothing touches my soul.[21]

The great mystic himself was abandoned at his time of his greatest need. But I am no great mystic, and if that's the price, I have no wish to be. The general rule for the likes of me is that God is there.

"Do not be afraid," said St. Brendan. "You will suffer no evil. Help for the journey is upon us."[22] The help is sometimes spectacular. The life of the Irish saint, St. Kevin of Glendalough, tells us about two female pilgrims to St. Kevin's church. They were ambushed by robbers in a remote pass, stripped, and beheaded. When the news reached Kevin, he rushed out to where their bodies were lying and, in the power of the Holy Spirit, reattached their heads to their trunks and brought them back to life.

Mostly, though, the help will be quieter. Until your ear gets attuned to the quiet cadences of God, you will probably call it coincidence. Whole books are now written on it: the big books call it *synchronicity*. It means that when you really need something, and often when you really want something, it is there. It is rightly said that when you pray, coincidences happen. When you walk as a pilgrim along a kingdom road, where every step is a prayer, coincidences happen too. We shouldn't be surprised. That's how we are told it will be. If we ask, it will be given.[23] All things work together for good for the people of God,[24] although it doesn't always seem like that at the time.

The needs are particularly urgent on the road, and particularly obviously met. That is just one reason why pilgrimage can be faith-building. Your vulnerability will be rewarded. The greater the vulnerability, the greater the reward. If you have nowhere to stay but press on anyway, someone is likely to come out for a smoke at twilight and offer you a barn to doss down in. If your feet are raw because you walked slightly farther and faster to stay with someone who needed you, at the next inn will be a plastic surgeon with an enormous supply of sophisticated dressings. The "Peace Pilgrim," who wandered around America

for twenty-eight years until her death in 1982, made this dependence an absolute rule. She never asked for anything; everything
necessary was given without asking. She walked until she was
offered a roof and a bed; she fasted until a stranger gave her food.
If you have hungered and thirsted after righteousness, don't be
surprised at the opulence of the party that is thrown for you.

Yes, you'll be guided, but not necessarily to the destination
you mapped out on the coffee table at home. "God takes your
hand and guides you in the darkness as though you were blind,"
wrote John of the Cross, "to an end and by a way which you
know not nor could you ever hope to travel with the aid of your
own eyes and feet, howsoever good you may be as a walker."[25]
Don't look too much at the compass. You are there to learn that
you don't need it. The weaning might be gentle, but it might
be firm. "Is not the all-powerful God the pilot and sailor of our
boat?" asked St. Brendan, who ought to know. "Leave it to him.
He himself guides our journey as he wills."[26]

On a road in northern India once, I met a stick-legged *sannyasi* clad in saffron, who rattled his begging bowl at me. "Some
rice, perhaps?" he said, in a cultivated accent (he turned out
to have an astrophysics PhD from Princeton). I gave him some.

"Where are you going?" I asked.

"To die, of course, just like you."

"And where will that be?"

"No idea. It will happen when it happens. I have no idea
where I am now."

And he didn't. He thought he was about three hundred miles from where he actually was.

Not all of us are that brave. But we can aspire.

"The beginning of the adventure of finding yourself is to lose your way," wrote Joseph Campbell.[27] He was right, but there is more to it than that. Meister Eckhart understood. For him, life and the pilgrim road were "the Wayless Way, where the Sons of God lose themselves and, at the same time, find themselves."[28]

11

THE FELLOWSHIP OF THE ROAD

I believe in the communion of saints.

—THE APOSTLES' CREED

The Lord . . . sent them on . . . in pairs.

—LUKE 10:1

I began to talk to everything along the Road; tree trunks, puddles, fallen leaves, and beautiful vines. It was an exercise of the common people, learned by children and forgotten by adults. And I received a mysterious response from these things, as if they understood what I was saying; they, in turn, flooded me with the love that consumes.

—PAULO COELHO[1]

MANY OF US, PARTICULARLY IN THE WEST, HAVE A HEROIC, individualistic view of pilgrimage. The picture in our heads is of a steep and remote mountain pass. We see ourselves, depending on our psychological makeup, either at the foot of the climb or at the summit. If we are male, we are ruggedly unshaven, and there is probably some blood caked on our knees. If we are female, we look engagingly windswept, but our nail polish is miraculously preserved. In either case the jaw is grimly, if winsomely, set. There is a long road ahead. We are here to do serious business with the universe. We will wrestle demons, orcs, and trolls to the ground; we will penetrate Indiana Jones–like to the hidden places of God and our own psyches. It's the view that the over-mocked pilgrim knight Don Quixote had of himself:

> *The world will be better for this,*
> *That one man, scorned and covered with scars*
> *Still strove, with his last ounce of courage,*
> *To reach the unreachable star.*[2]

The picture would be wrecked by a gaggle of giggling, anorak-swathed Swedes eating egg sandwiches. Yet it is the Swedes and their sandwiches that are the main vehicles of grace. Many pilgrimages (and the best ones) start as solitary endeavors. Most end in a party. It is pilgrims who make a pilgrimage: "Looking back on it, I feel really shallow," said Kate, who had walked from Canterbury to Santiago in the wake of her husband's death.

I went with a thick, leather-bound journal, in which I was going to plumb the secrets of myself, and rail at God, and hopefully learn to bless him. I was going to write dark, cynical, clever poems in the style of Auden and Yeats, and do neat little watercolours of mountains and monasteries. People were going to think that I was so brave, and grudgingly, graciously, I was going to agree with them. Probably with tears.

But it didn't happen that way. I have the journal, and it is one of my most treasured possessions. But the only poem in it is a limerick that I'd be embarrassed for my children to read (they're very proper). There is one watercolour of a sheep, and a Spanish plumber I met in Leon has drawn an arrow through its head. There are some pressed flowers. But the rest of the journal is full of email addresses and phone numbers. I wasn't brave at all. From the start the whole thing was a hoot. I walked in a shifting party of merry-makers. We'd sing, laugh, gather up followers on the way, hilariously misunderstand what we were saying, but somehow get the point, and a deeper point, too, and buy the cheapest red wine we could find.

Kate wasn't shallow at all. She had discovered the communion of the saints, a communion that survives death and seems to transcend species. Nomads are an intimate family. Every one can say, "A wandering Aramean was my ancestor,"[3] so they are siblings. They have their own family language. A strange, amusing sort of gift of tongues is given to the guests around a pilgrim table. A German finds that he is eloquent and funny to monolingual Finns. A rudimentary sort of telepathy begins to operate, as it operates precisely and importantly between those Kalahari hunters.

The intimacy is both a consequence and a cause of the freedom the road gives. There is no need to pretend to be anything with these people. That is terribly rare. But a man who couldn't care less what other people think of him has colossal peace and power. There are few things he can't do. There is no peer pressure, because today's peers will be gone tomorrow or the day after, or if the pace is different, at the next step. And it is a community of equals. There are no bosses and no kings. Everyone walks, and no one eats unless he gets to the next farm.

In the freedom the road gives, you can be yourself, probably for the first time since you were a very young child. "Think of how free I am," said the Peace Pilgrim. "If I want to travel, I just stand up and walk away." She was far freer than any queen. This means that the relationships you make on the road are with real people. This is highly unusual and immensely exhilarating. Normally there is reserve and caution. Back at home you think you are friends with John. He thinks he's friends with you. But are you really? How can you be? John doesn't have the first idea who he is himself, and so he can't offer himself to you in friendship. The John you think you know is a complex amalgam of things: a managing director, a husband, a frustrated novelist, a hypochondriac specializing in bowel cancer, a debtor, an occasional opportunistic adulterer, and a teacher at Sunday school. How does God know what to save? How do we know what there is to know? Who is there?

On the road, though, it is different. John will already have jettisoned lots of stuff. He has left the managing directorship behind and shredded his work suit. He has repented of his flings with overly receptive receptionists, and he will let the children teach him in future at Sunday school. He got drunk in a field and laughed for the first time in a decade without worrying whether the incident would find its way onto his appraisal. He then found himself crying and making his peace with his long-dead mother. He woke up with a splitting headache, a desire to find his old infant school teacher and thank her, and a curious thirst for the Psalms. A woman with MS fed him tortilla and aspirin from a tin plate, and he kissed her on the cheek. He was beginning to be a person that someone could know. Relationship was possible again. The two divine processes of sloughing and integration were galloping through him.

Bunyan gets another thing badly wrong. Mr. Talkative comes alongside Christian and Faithful, and Faithful suggests, gnostically and boringly, that they talk "of things that are profitable." Mr. Talkative, for Bunyan an unhappy example of another of the road's deadly hazards, boasts of his ability to talk about anything: "I will talk of things heavenly, or things earthly; things sacred or things profane; things past, or things to come; things foreign, or things at home." "Good for him," should be the response, but of course it isn't.[4]

When Mr. Talkative comes up to you on the Kentish Downs outside Canterbury, encourage him to talk. It is kind and will probably be interesting. You'll learn a lot, and he'll learn a lot from being listened to. If he's full of nonsense, let it spew out onto the roadside verge. The road will point out the contrast between his absurdities and the realities that will be assailing him on his pilgrimage. His garrulousness might be part of the sloughing process: he might be getting rid of the last bit of the office-man. It's a privilege to be the stone on which he grinds off the old coat. On an Alpha course, sit and listen with respect and love to people's extraordinary stories. It is unusual for anyone to listen to anyone else with full attention and respect. Model God's unconditional acceptance and love for them and for you.

And don't just talk to the humans.

"A really strange thing happened when I was about halfway to Santiago," said Kate. "I'm embarrassed to tell you about it." She blushed and squirmed. "I started talking to the trees and the birds," she said. "It wasn't a pose, and I'm not insane. It would have seemed rude not to. I was on their patch, and they were the hosts. They seemed to appreciate it. Sometimes I even thought that they replied."

I can't put that into a book on pilgrimage, I thought. *I really can't.* But then other pilgrims started to say similar things, and it seemed I had to deal with it. After all, what is the theological problem? The pilgrimage road is part of the kingdom. People are following Jesus along it, and as he walks, he proclaims at every step, "The kingdom of God has come near."[5] In that kingdom, the old animosities between the species are healed. Isaiah 11:6 foresees the ecological consequences: the wolf will live with the lamb, the leopard shall lie down with the kid, and animals generally won't be as scared rigid of that most brutal, indiscriminate, genocidal killer, *Homo sapiens*, as history has taught them to be. Who knows how the first fruits of that reconciliation might look and taste?[6] If someone tried to get Kate slung into a psychiatric ward or dismissed from the roll of elders at her church (presumably on the grounds of sinister pantheistic tendencies), she could call some very impressive witnesses in her defense. "Wait for me," said St. Francis, when he was on pilgrimage with his friends. "I must go to preach to my sisters the birds." And that is exactly what he did. The birds listened, enraptured, to his sermon: "Consider the birds."[7] He persuaded the man-eating wolf of Gubbio to behave himself. And then there is St. Cuthbert of Lindisfarne. Eider ducks flew to him, seals played with him on the beach, and otters ran out of the surf to warm his feet. Even the bacteria involved in the decomposition of dead flesh were his friends: when his coffin was opened, eleven years after his death, his body was as fresh as the day he died. The guardian of the shrine trimmed the saint's nails and "the ever-growing hair of his venerable beard." When Vikings murdered St. Edmund, his murderers cut off his head and hid it in a wood. His friends, searching for the head, heard a voice calling from the wood, "Here, here, here." They found a wolf guarding the head. It trotted calmly after them as they took the head off for burial. Ravens stopped wild animals from eating the body of the murdered St. Vincent.

This will go far too far for most people. I'm not sure that it doesn't go too far for me. All I say is that there is a consistent tradition in the church of such things, and it's not necessarily theological gibberish.

When you go on your pilgrimage, don't feel you have to talk to the cows. But don't feel inhibited either. The most important thing is to know and to experience the truth of that ancient pilgrimage song of Israel in Psalm 133, sung as the pilgrims made their way to the Jerusalem temple: "How very good and pleasant it is, when kindred live together in unity!" That was a firsthand observation of what happens on pilgrimage. Divisions are bridged: race, status, and gender are irrelevant. As New Testamental people, we understand even more of what the song meant. In each other and in the waifs and strays en route, pilgrims meet the king. Where he is, there is the kingdom as he promised. And the kingdom is a place of perfect, unsullied community—that great city with the intimacy of the roadside campfire.

But it doesn't do to get too romantic. It's not always like that. Good though pilgrimage is at stamping out bigotry and general tiresomeness, it is not infallible.

Perhaps my experience is jaundiced, but I have found that the more overtly religious someone is, the more tedious is his company, the more useless and selfish he is, and the more unpopular he is. I've had far more buns and bandages from secular humanists than from passionate advocates of the Tridentine Mass or loud denouncers of the pope as Anti-Christ.

Perhaps the most reviled pilgrim of all time was the most

religious: Margery Kempe. In 1411 she was convinced that God was calling her on pilgrimage. She gave up sex with her husband, saying that she would rather be dead than that they should "turn again to [their] uncleanness," and, waving good-bye to him and her children, set off in 1413 for the Holy Land. In Rome, her fellow pilgrims were upset by her grotesque religious enthusiasm. She wept constantly, not stopping while she ate, and reminding everyone who would listen, and everyone else, of the "love and goodness of our Lord." The group tried to shake her off, but she clung to them like an evangelical limpet all the way to Jerusalem. There things went from bad to worse. At Calvary, in the Church of the Holy Sepulchre, she fell down and rolled around, thrashing, shouting out pieties. She noted, as if she had done her bit for God, that people were astounded by the volume. She rode sobbing into Bethlehem, and that was the last straw for her patient fellow travelers. They refused to eat with her. She continued to weep her way to Rome, dressed now in white. Perhaps the psychiatrists of K'far Shmuel would have diagnosed Jerusalem Syndrome, but it didn't quite fit: she was strange long before she climbed the final rise from the plain of Sharon.[8] She returned to England for a short time, and was then off again, this time to Santiago, wielding her customary handkerchief and her selfish, intrusive, irritating sanctimony. Gnostics, when all is said and done, are a real pain. Pilgrimage seems to have taught her nothing.

Medieval pilgrims were usually men of their time, and when the times were times of schism and sectarianism, pilgrimage often did not achieve what it usually achieves now—ecumenical respect. As those armed pilgrims, the crusaders, marched toward Jerusalem, they murdered and plundered Jews and the Orthodox. Pietro Casola in 1494 noted with wonder the variety of denominations to be found in Jerusalem, but commented that they "have a very strange way of chanting the offices . . . which rather provoked the company to laughter."[9] The German Dominican monk Felix Fabri, who reached Mount Sinai in 1483, couldn't decide whom he despised more, Muslims or non-Catholic Christians. When he was unable to attend Mass in the Orthodox chapel, he gave thanks to the benevolent God, "which would not suffer us to celebrate Mass in a schismatical or heretical church" presided over by "excommunicate" monks.[10]

"I hear that some of this church is owned by Christians, and some by the Greek Orthodox," said a young, fleshy man from Alabama in the Chapel of the Finding of the Cross in the Holy Sepulchre.

That sort of apartheid is perpetuated today not primarily in attitudes (although it is there still, of course), but in separate itineraries. Protestants in Jerusalem may decide that the Garden Tomb, rather than the Church of the Holy Sepulchre, contains the tomb of Jesus, and so cut themselves off from the most consistent tradition of the church, going back to before the time of Helena. They often won't be challenged by the archaeological realities or the sight of real, unfakeable ardor from Catholics, Orthodox, and many others. They will stay in separate hotels.

They will be carefully cocooned by their pastors from contamination (also known as cross-fertilization) by other, older traditions. It's a terrible shame. If you go to Rome, go to Rome; don't import a little corner of Idaho onto Italian territory.

It's not just pilgrims who make a pilgrimage: it's pilgrims different from you. A pilgrimage is a journey to the ultimate *otherness*. Navigating there will be a lot easier if you travel in a shoal of other othernesses. In the course of it, you will become ever more completely yourself, but that happens not by navel-gazing or the cozy affirmation of the people you've selected over years because they agree with you, but by meeting the gaze of Jesus in the strangers on the road.

12

ARRIVAL AND RETURN

*I was glad when they said to me, "Let us go to the house of
the LORD!" Our feet are standing within your gates, O Jerusalem.*

—PSALM 122:1–2

*Then said [Mr. Valiant-for-Truth], "I am going to my Father's; and
though with great difficulty I have got hither, yet now I do not repent me
of all the trouble I have been at to arrive where I am. My sword I give to
him that shall succeed me in my pilgrimage, and my courage and skill to
him that can get it. My marks and scars I carry with me, to be a witness
for me that I have fought His battles who will now be my rewarder."
When the day that he must go hence was come, many accompanied him to
the river-side, into which as he went, he said, "Death, where is thy sting?"
And as he went down deeper, he said, "Grave, where is thy victory?" So he
passed over, and all the trumpets sounded for him on the other side.*

—JOHN BUNYAN, *PILGRIM'S PROGRESS*[1]

*The point of travelling is not to arrive, but to return home laden with
pollen you shall work up into the honey the mind feeds on.*

—R. S. THOMAS [2]

SO YOU'VE FOLLOWED THE LOPING, HOMELESS MAN-GOD to Jerusalem. Now what? You went, encouraged by the tales of people who had gone before you, expecting an encounter. There have been plenty of encounters along the road. You have met yourself too. Is that it?

"Yes, I suppose I wanted an encounter," said Ruth, "but I also wanted answers. Sometimes it seemed as if I wanted an encounter only because it might be with somebody or something that could give me answers."

Perhaps every pilgrimage is a journey to an oracle. There is a lot of competition in the oracle market.

Nobody finds answers in Jerusalem, unless the question is, "Is it really that simple?" To that, the answer is consistent and emphatic: "Yes, repeat No." We all come here expecting to find answers, but we come back again and again because we get addicted to doubt and uncertainty.

The place taunts. It should be so easy. There is no huge haystack through which to search for the needle of wisdom. It taunts by the apparent accessibility of wisdom. So do the other shrines. You want to be physically in contact with St. Paul? Easy. Go to his grave in the Basilica of San Paulo in Rome, which is like a mosque without the carpets or the gravitas, or a fake Baroque airport-arrivals hall. The grave is a flash of real rock in the middle—the only thing there I could believe in. Get in line. Pray there. You're in touch. But it doesn't feel like that.

The taunt of Jerusalem is particularly cruel. Standing on the terrace above the Western Wall plaza, you can see just about everything that matters to Judaism, many of the tangled roots of Christianity, and a sacred shrine of Islam. Indeed the real nursery of Islam is here. Beyond the lights of Silwan is a low, dark curve, like the flank of a lion—the desert, which howls and ripples, a place of teeth and hot dreams.

If the rabbis are right, the Temple Mount is Mount Moriah, where Abraham's terrible obedience convinced Yahweh that he should enter a binding contract with the offspring of the near murderer and the near victim. It was here, in the stinking dark of the Holy of Holies, behind a curtain, that the blood of bulls and goats traced out some sort of metaphysical ladder up which men tottered uncertainly toward God. It is a strange metaphysics that needs its plans sketched and its axioms built in blood.

When the temple fell the first time, it was a catastrophe. "How could we sing the LORD's song in a foreign land?"[3] the Jews asked from Babylon. They couldn't. Not because the Lord did not rule in Babylon; on the contrary, he seemed most emphatically to do so. Not because he had lost his ear for his people's songs; he longed to hear them. And not because Babylon was a long way from Jerusalem; it was, but the psalms of exile were not homesick whining. They were the panic-filled screams of a people who had lost access to the source of their being. To be away from Jerusalem was bad enough, but Jerusalem was only home because it was the way Home. Jerusalem without the temple was another, perhaps more poignant, sort of exile.

So the temple was rebuilt. The ladder was remade. The ascent resumed. For a while.

And then a man appeared who said, with monstrous audacity, that he was the temple and that soon he would be the only temple. Whether or not he was right, Romans razed the temple in AD 70, wrecking the old ladder.

This man had a strange relationship with the stones of Jerusalem. "If the people are quiet," he proclaimed on the way to his murder, "the stones themselves will sing."[4] There is no theological reason to suppose they have lost their voice. Quieter pilgrims still listen for it.

Most of the Jews did not believe that the man was the temple. And they had a problem. There was now no temple. They were dispersed to ten thousand Babylons. And there, in a way that I do not understand, they learned to sing the Lord's song in a strange land after all. But to put it at its lowest, that song does not have the resonance given it by the extraordinary spiritual acoustic of Solomon, or even the grand but tinnier notes of Herod. It was not a joy-song for the redeemed. It was now in an intoxicating minor key. It went on for so long and was sung by such brilliant singers, that the world began to think that beauty and meaning had to be conveyed in a minor key; that the ecstatic, summery songs of ascent, which tell of flowers and the smiles of children, are shallow and tawdry; that those songs have missed the point.

It was a Friday night. The yeshiva boys danced to the Wall in their best suits, as if to a wedding, to greet their Lady Shabbat (Sabbath). The Wall is part of the retaining wall of the Herodian Temple Mount. On the top of the platform, more or less where the two previous temples stood, is the Dome of the Rock, built there very soon after the Islamic conquest of Palestine to make the point, in thousands of tons of gorgeous masonry, mosaic, and gold, for anyone dumb enough to have missed it: Islam was built on the rubble of the Judeo-Christian tradition; the teachings of Moses and Jesus had to be read through the lens handed to history by the prophet Mohammed.

And nothing much has changed since the conquest. There is no new temple. If history is the judge, Islam has the verdict. What can the yeshiva boys have to sing about?

They meet with Lady Shabbat, but surely she mocks them. She marks yet another week without the means of redemption. The boys are themselves being deceitful. The songs are not really to Lady Shabbat but to another sacred Lady. She clings to the wall and whispers between the cracks. I have heard her best in the dead of night or the very early morning. The rabbis are very clear about her gender. She is the Lady Shekinah, the holy presence of Yahweh. She lived in the holy of holies and has never quite abandoned the Temple Mount. Once she threw wild parties in the temple with trumpeters and roast oxen. Now she is a wraith. Yahweh is male, but his presence is so female that all femininity is only feminine insofar as it approaches her.

On roads, on planes, on ships, over icy passes, and through pressing crowds, we have followed a Man whose resurrection body is so solid that it passes effortlessly through walls, and whose Bacchanalian tastes are so strong that he tells us to remember him when we drink wine. He has led us to a strange encounter with a shadowy, fickle, whispering woman. Sometimes she can be heard above the wail of the muezzin, the murmur of Hebrew prayers, the moan of the wind from Arabia, and the brass bands celebrating the commissioning of Israeli paratroopers. But often she cannot. It's a weird way for God to behave. It's almost as if he is playing hide-and-seek with us. Some do not share my difficulties. Some have talked, at least, as if Jerusalem has been the consummation they have devoutly sought.

In AD 385, Jerome went to Palestine with a Roman woman, Paula, and her daughter. Paula was ecstatic in the holy places. "So great was the passion and the enthusiasm she exhibited for each," wrote Jerome, "that she could never have torn herself away from one had she not been eager to visit the rest. Before the cross she threw herself down in adoration as though she beheld the Lord hanging upon it, and when she entered the tomb which was the scene of the resurrection, she kissed the stone which the angel had rolled away from the door of the sepulchre."

In Bethlehem she thought she saw with the "eyes of her soul" the baby Jesus, crying in the manger.[5]

Occasionally dramatic things happen at the destination. Mary, a fifth-century prostitute from Alexandria, financed her trip to the Holy Land by plying her trade all the way from Egypt. Then an invisible force prevented her from entering the Church of the Holy Sepulchre. Terrified, she repented, and is now known to history as St. Mary of Egypt, one of the great desert saints. The Russian abbot Daniel, who visited the Holy Land in 1106–8, noted that "no one can hold back tears at the sight of that desired land [Jerusalem] and the holy places where Christ our God suffered his passion for the sake of us sinners. And all go on foot in great joy towards the city."[6]

Felix Fabri, the friar who reached Jerusalem in the late fifteenth century, wrote movingly about how he prayed on "the Holy Hill of Calvary" for all the people on his heart, evidently convinced that prayers there would be particularly efficacious. "I went with the paper [on which their names were written] to the holy rock, and there, kneeling on my knees, I laid that paper on the holy rock and offered a prayer for each person."[7] (Nowadays you can e-mail your prayers to a Jewish organization in Jerusalem. The e-mail is printed off and put in one of the cracks of the Western Wall.)

But it is hard to find ecstatic accounts of arrival at the major Christian pilgrimage sites. There is rarely regret about going; all the travelers think it has been worthwhile; but unless there has been a specific miracle (such as one of the healing miracles often reported from Lourdes and elsewhere), there may be an undercurrent of disappointment—a disappointment that cannot be voiced, because it would seem to be rather blasphemous or because it would throw open the door to paralyzing, faith-destroying doubt. Jerome's Roman woman seems to be trying a bit too hard to be moved. Daniel wipes his tears quickly away and moves on to write a report of his travels filled with measurements, architectural details, and rather obvious sermonizing. He's more of a quantity surveyor than a mystic. Felix Fabri's account speaks of duty rather than epiphany. If epiphanies happen, they tend to happen in the anonymous no-man's-lands en route.

This disappointment is seen in the fables about the Holy Land that erupted and persisted in the Middle Ages. The map wrongly attributed to William Wey points out the river that only gushes out of the ground on the Day of Epiphany, and a wood where all the birds die on Passion Sunday but revive on Easter Sunday. You only invent extravagant marvels if the real historical ones haven't come up to scratch. "More," the legends say. "We want more." The pilgrims are still thirsty. Jerusalem has failed.

Some faithful, fearful, faith-guarding pilgrims found that Jerusalem disappointed because it stubbornly failed to conform to their cherished ideas about the world. William Wey soberly and honestly noted that the alleged footprints of the ascending Christ on the summit of the Mount of Olives were more likely to be genuine than the ones shown to him in Westminster. But to conclude that the Westminster ones were bogus would be to loosen the mortar of a whole precious edifice of belief about other shrines and relics. And so he doesn't—it seems that he can't—go so far. He moves on, holding in dangerous tension in his head two entirely contradictory ideas. It's a very common modern state. He's in a state of cognitive dissonance, and more than halfway to wrapping himself up in a sheet and proclaiming that the end of the world is nigh.

Other travelers had no qualms about voicing their disappointment. "All is glitter and nothing is gold," wrote Herman Melville of the Church of the Holy Sepulchre. "A sickening cheat. The countenances of the poorest and most ignorant pilgrims would seem tacitly to confess it as well as your own."[8] W. H. Bartlett was no more impressed: "Nothing can be more dull than the view within the city—the high, dead walls of the Armenian convent, broken ground covered with rubbish, and the half-ruinous houses of the Jewish Quarter keep up the impression of melancholy that rarely quits the mind of the sojourner in the City of David."[9]

It's not just Jerusalem that disappoints: it is arrival in general. One of the best modern pilgrimage accounts is that of an English woman, Caroline Friend, who walked the Chemin St. Jacques to Santiago after a series of family tragedies.[10] It's a glorious, luminescent story, full of hope and laughter. She can certainly write about deep and high experiences. "When we were blessed at Conques [about a third of the way along], I was in tears at the beauty of the service and at the intensity with which the abbot prayed for us. I found myself actually sinking to my knees in the middle of the path to thank God for everything he was giving me, from wild figs for my lunch to fellow pilgrims who were more loving and more generous than I had any right to expect." And yet there's not a single word— not one—about Santiago. The general tone is that arrival is no arrival at all: it's a start.

Shirley du Boulay walked from Winchester to Canterbury: "This pilgrimage . . . had not ended on arrival any more than life ends with death. But I did feel that I understood better where the sacred place is found."[11]

Even for those who do experience some sort of consummation, the consummation is not an end but a beginning: "Looking at these figures, I was suddenly, almost forcibly, jerked clean out of the habitual, half-tied vision of things, and an inner clearness, clarity, as if exploding from the rocks themselves, became evident and obvious," wrote the American Trappist monk Thomas Merton.

I don't know when in my life I have ever had such a sense of beauty and spiritual validity running together in one aesthetic illumination. Surely with Mahabalipuram and Polonnaruwa my Asia pilgrimage has come clear and purified itself. I mean,

I know and have seen what I was obscurely looking for. I don't know what else remains, but I have now seen and have pierced through the surface and have got beyond the shadow and disguise.[12]

The preliminaries are over. The darkness has cleared. It is time to *begin*.

The Brazilian writer Paulo Coelho was about to have his sword given to him as a mark of graduation in a magical order. At the last moment it was snatched from him, and he was ordered to go on the pilgrimage to Santiago de Compostela. Somewhere on the road, he thought, *I will find my sword*. It proved elusive. And then the doors were flung open. The purpose of his pilgrimage was to make him ask the question, "What am I going to use my sword for?" Having a sword is pointless unless you have asked and answered that question.

And that is why you have to go back home.

Pilgrimage changes people. It often changes their houses. Sue, who had walked from London to Rome across the St. Bernard's Pass, plastered her kitchen with photos of the people she had met and the sites she had seen. William Wey, back from Jerusalem, built a chapel at his Wiltshire Retreat and turned it into a sacred museum. There, every day, piously and oddly, he prayed at and stroked the stones he had brought from Calvary and Mount

Tabor, the board he had carefully marked with various holy dimensions, including the size of Jesus' feet, a replica of the mortise stone at the foot of the cross, and his wooden models of the Calvary Chapel and the Church of the Nativity. Although Wey tells us very little about the end of his life, I am sure that if asked to summarize his career as he lay dying in 1476, he would have gasped out, "I'm William Wey, pilgrim."

Other pilgrims want to mark themselves out as pilgrims, to say, "This is what I am." The mark might be the saffron robe of the *sannyasi*, the cockleshell of the Santiago pilgrim, the dyed beard of the *hajii* who has completed the pilgrimage to Mecca, or one of the pilgrim badges that were sold in colossal numbers from the early Middle Ages onward.

William Wey and Sue wanted to import some of the holiness they had found—on the journey, if not at the destination. Holiness, in this gleefully physical world of ours, can travel in pebbles or trinkets. Or perhaps, since they had had an encounter, they wanted some physical confirmation of it, like an engagement ring. The Welsh poet R. S. Thomas talked about a desire for "something to bring back to show you have been there; a lock of God's hair, stolen from him while he was asleep; a photograph of the garden of the spirit."[13]

Christianity, though, is not magic. To wield an olive-wood cross bought in Jerusalem as if it were an enchanted amulet is to misunderstand. Yes, Jerusalem, Rome, and Santiago are special places. There's no heresy in admitting it. But that doesn't mean the specialness (as opposed to a memory of the specialness) can be brought away in your backpack. The stones of Jerusalem are special because they are in Jerusalem. To worship them in a Wiltshire chapel might not only be foolish, but dangerously foolish. Some of the old legends seem to recognize this. When, on the way back to Venice from Jaffa, there was a suspected case of plague on Pietro Casola's boat, the captain ordered all water from the river Jordan thrown overboard. It brought health and healing when drunk in the Holy Land, but it became unlucky elsewhere. The tale hints that holiness isn't a commodity that can be exported like oranges. To have Jordan water on tap in Venice is an attempt to pretend that you are still in the Holy Land, that you're not really in Venice.

Departure is crucial. Home is the part of the kingdom where you will wield your sword. You have to leave Jerusalem properly in order to be able to wield your sword properly.

The writer Phil Cousineau (not a Christian) notes that the big difficulty for the returning pilgrim is how to keep the "sacred memories" alive:

> How to make the journey part of our lives once we are back in the daily grind? I see the time of return as a reintegration time, a time to recall as much as possible about the trip, a time of listening to dreams and creating something new *so the awakening continues*. This is so important because you've changed. Something shifted and came to consciousness. Now

you know the sacred is everywhere. Now you know the miniature is inside you."[14]

This is wise advice. The Christian should have an advantage, though. He knows very well, and on authority far higher than the experience of his own trip to a desert monastery, that the sacred seeps everywhere. He knows, too, that it is unevenly distributed; there is a lot more of it in homeless shelters than on Wall Street. He knows that the flowers of the kingdom spring up at the feet of the man who couldn't care less what others think of him; that you find truth and life when you are on a *Way*; that in order to be first, you have to be last.

Jesus traveled all the time and talked a lot about travel. But arrival? For him, too, arrivals were always starts.

The parable of the prodigal son is a travel story.[15] The son goes roaming, and it doesn't make him happy because he's roaming in a squalid place. We don't hear much about it, and we don't need to. The really explicit travel tale is the tale of the return. It's a tale of two travelers. The son's back on the right road. It is a road to an end that will be a beginning. The father sees his son coming and rushes out to hug him. The ending will be a start for both of them.

Going back probably won't be easy. "Prophets are not without honor except in their own country and in their own house," Jesus warned.[16] We might have cited that in support of the suggestion that the best course is always to get up and go. But now it seems, in the light of the other things we've seen, the whole teaching is, "Get up and go; come back and wield your sword in the part of the kingdom where you can wield it best. But don't expect an easy time if that part happens to be where you're from. If you've been changed by the road as you should have been, all the stay-at-homes are going to be appalled when you tell them tales about the wild kingdom where top is bottom and the poor are rich, and they won't take kindly to your telling them that's how they have to live in order to be happy and properly safe."

After his sweat-stained, fly-swatting, foot-cracked trail-life in the dust and grit of the Near East, the hiking God made his way through the hills to Jerusalem. The roads would have been busy; it was peak pilgrimage season. It was a journey home. He had been born just a few miles away in Bethlehem, and the temple was the house of the old tribal deity he called father. Betrayed by a fellow traveler, his journey seemed to end. But things are not always what they seem. Indeed, in the weird kingdom that Jesus spoke of, things are never as they seem. Three days later there was apparently a great beginning.

"The pilgrimage changed me forever," said Sue.

I met myself, and learned to love myself. I'm told to love

others as I love myself. And so, when I'm obedient to that command, I love others better too. I left behind lots of things that weren't me, but which I had stupidly thought were central parts of who I was. There's one thing that I'm not sure about, though. I don't know if I was really a pilgrim before and simply discovered that on the journey, or whether the journey turned me into a pilgrim. Perhaps it doesn't matter; whatever's the truth, I now know that deep at the heart of what I am and am meant to be, I am a pilgrim.

13

"IT'S A PROFANE JOURNEY": OPPONENTS OF PILGRIMAGE

Sometimes, reading the literature, particularly maybe the later Protestant pilgrims, you're wandering through a vinegar factory.

—Dennis Silk[1]

They are deluded by an ignorant blind zeal and are to be pitied by us that have the advantage of knowing better and ought to be pitied.

—Celia Fiennes [2]

Hari dwells in the East, they say, and Allah resides in the west. Search for him in your heart, in the heart of your heart.

—Kabir, fifteenth-century North Indian mystic [3]

"All pilgrimages should be stopped," thundered Martin Luther, a man never short on certainty. "There is no good in them: no commandment enjoins them, no obedience attaches to them. Rather do pilgrimages give countless occasions to commit sin and to despise God's commandments."[4] Legend gives pilgrimage a central and dishonorable place in the history of the Reformation. While he was crawling devoutly up the Scala Santa in Rome in 1510, goes the story, Luther heard a voice saying, "The just shall live by faith; not by pilgrimage, and not by penance." The scales cascaded from Luther's eyes. He stood up, walked back down, and stalked out to ignite the Reformation.

Luther was neither the first nor the last to denounce pilgrimage (although he may have been the loudest). Many reasons have been advanced for decrying the practice. The Lollards and many of the Reformers thought the emphasis in many pilgrimages on relics was diabolical superstition, and objected to the often-obscene profits generated by the big pilgrimage centers. "God," said Wycliffe, "gave his sheep to be pastured, not to be shaven and shorn."[5] Many were skeptical of the cult of saints in general. "Why St. Thomas [of Canterbury] rather than St. Robin Hood?" asked William Umpton in 1530, a question on which he had plenty of time to ruminate, since he was handed into the Tower of London in irons for asking it.[6] Pilgrimage has played a predictable role in the iconoclastic controversies that have periodically rocked the church since soon after its birth. How can miracles be worked by "dead images?" asked John Foxe, in his 1563 *Book of Martyrs*, echoing a phrase that has reverberated tediously and bloodily through Christendom for millennia. Mere politics have often affected the pilgrimage market. When Henry VIII got jumpy about criticism of his monarchy by the church, he suppressed pilgrimage to Canterbury, thinking it might not be wise to invite devotion to the saint who had died asserting that the church should trump the crown.

Other opponents declared, as Luther almost did, that pilgrimages should be stopped because they were fun.[7] Here is William Thorpe, a man who doesn't sound like a great dinner-party guest, writing in 1407:

> [Pilgrimages] have with them both men and women that can sing wanton songs, and some other pilgrims will have with them bagpipes, so that every town that they come through, what with the noise of their singing, and with the sound of their piping, and with the jangling of their Canterbury bells, and with the barking of dogs after them, they make more noise than if the king came their way with all his clarions and many other minstrels.[8]

Often theological bigotry, cultural ignorance, and life-denying Puritanism come unattractively together.

"Just look at them," said a large lady from Brisbane in elastic-waisted trousers. And I did. What I saw was an exuberant procession through the streets of a southern Italian town of a statue of the Black Madonna. She was borne on the shoulders of twenty men, all in their best suits. Fireworks spurted, swallows dived, glasses clinked, girls winked, and a nun waltzed with a policeman. Slaughtered sheep rotated over a driftwood fire, and the air was thick with rosemary. As the Madonna passed, an old woman limped over and pushed past the bearers to touch her dress. She threw away her stick and shouted, "I'm healed!" The crowd cheered, and the old woman was hoisted up onto a balcony. She took off her pearl necklace, ripped the string, and flung the pearls into the crowd, screaming, "For you, Mother Mary!"

I had walked for three days to get there, sleeping rough. On the last day, I had met a group of students from Bari, also walking to the festival. One of the boys from the group poured some local wine into a plastic cup and offered it to the American lady. She scowled at him, muttered, "Disgusting," and knocked it out of his hand. The red stain spread across his T-shirt like blood. He laughed and kissed her on the cheek. She screamed, and he laughed more. "Let me go," she spluttered. "This superstition. This idolatry. This demonic filth." She swam through the press of happy bodies and back to the minibus that had brought her from Naples. She was the adventurous, liberal one. The others in her party were hunched in the vehicle, praying that the town would be delivered from the clutch of Satan.

But the main justification advanced by the denouncers is that pilgrimages are theologically unnecessary, and if you can be bothered to go on one, you must have made the dangerous theological mistake of thinking they are necessary.

A ninth-century Irish abbot wrote:

> *Who to Rome goes,*
> *Much labour, little profit knows;*

For God, on earth though long you've sought him,
You'll miss in Rome, unless you've brought him.[9]

"So why bother?" asks the abbot. I have to say I don't share the experience of that gloomy, earnest abbot. "When you search for me, you will find me; if you seek me with all your heart, I will let you find me, says the LORD," says Jeremiah.[10] Going to Rome, Geneva, or your own sacred mountain might well be part of that full-hearted searching.

"Why bother?" is the reasoning most commonly heard from religious but non-Christian writers. The great Sufi mystic Abu Said, born in 967, advised his followers to stay away from Mecca so they could work at home on achieving intimacy with God. "It is no great matter that you should walk a thousand miles in order to visit a stone house. The true man of God sits where he is, and the Bayt al-Ma'Mur [the heavenly Ka'aba] comes several times in a day and a night to visit him and performs the circumambulation above his head. Look and see!"[11]

In Hinduism, the Mahabharata, while laying down and recommending an exhausting itinerary of physical pilgrimages, emphasizes that the most important journey is the inward one. Yes, the *tirtha* (ritual bathing) that you do in Varanasi is significant, but the "*tirthas* of the heart," which you can do when you are spinning or eating dhal, are the most significant of all. The great mediaeval Hindu poet Kabir wrote wearily, "Going on endless pilgrimages, the world died, exhausted by so much bathing."[12]

In the Christian literature, there are some strange non sequiturs flying around. Jerome declared, "Access to the courts of heaven is as easy from Britain as it is from Jerusalem, for the Kingdom of God is within you."[13] *Fair enough*, you might think. But he goes on, as if it follows, "Nothing is lacking to your faith though you have not seen Jerusalem." I know that a lot would be lacking to my faith if I had not seen Jerusalem, just as a lot would be lacking to my faith if I had not met my friend David; or had not happened to be in the Royal Oak, Southwark, where there was a tangle-haired Irish girl; or had not, as a child, become a passionate naturalist. People with bodies are affected by the environments in which those bodies exist. It's hard to be too paranoid about all the toxic gnosticism sloshing around the church.

Many of the anti-pilgrimage comments are specific reactions to the abuses of the time. They cannot be generalized, and they do not justify abstaining from pilgrimage. When Gregory of Nyssa says, "When the Lord invites the blest to their inheritance in the Kingdom of Heaven, He does not include a pilgrimage to Jerusalem among their good deeds,"[14] we can agree with him that there is nothing *necessarily* good about a pilgrimage, but point out that many have been helped mightily by it. When the early Irish abbess Samthann tells us, "Since God is near to all who call upon him, we are under no obligation to cross the sea. The Kingdom of heaven can be reached from every land,"[15] we can say, "Fair enough. No theological obligation, certainly. The obligation comes from my heart, and needs to be taken seriously."

The Reformers did their best to shut down pilgrimage. In Protestant lands, aided by increasingly impervious national boundaries, they more or less succeeded. For a while. But they knew the incantatory power of pilgrimage language and sought to harness it to the thrusting engines of Protestant piety. John Bunyan's great book, *Pilgrim's Progress*, is the classic example. It is an illuminating irony that Bunyan himself, being both a creature and a tool of nonconformist orthodoxy, would probably have frowned hard at any actual pilgrims who trudged through his native Bedfordshire on the way to Walsingham or Canterbury. For him pilgrimage was a crucial metaphor, but only a metaphor. Real pilgrimages sullied the metaphor and were best avoided. Pilgrim's progress, the book carefully explains, was "from this world to that which is to come, delivered under the similitude of a Dream, wherein is discovered the manner of his setting out, his dangerous journey and safe arrival at the desired country."[16] But Bunyan was a shrewd writer. He knew that real, muddy, chafing, mile-eating pilgrimages were the best vehicle for the spiritual lessons he had to teach, and so he goes to great literary lengths to reproduce them. Trail-sweat runs from his pages. He even, arch-iconoclast though he was, bothers to have Christian visiting in the Palace Beautiful, and with very un-Protestant enthusiasm, a stupendous collection of relics that would have made any medieval pope green with envy:

They also shewed him some of the Engines with which some of his Servants had done wonderful things. They shewed him Moses' Rod; the Hammer and Nail with which Jael slew Sisera; the Pitchers, Trumpets and Lamps too, with which Gideon put to flight the Armies of Midian: Then they shewed him the Ox's goad wherewith Shamgar slew six hundred men: They shewed him also the Jawbone with which Samson did such mighty feats: They shewed him moreover the Sling and Stone with which David slew Goliath of Gath; and the Sword also with which their Lord will kill the Man of Sin, in the day that he shall rise up to the prey. They shewed him besides many excellent things, with which Christian was much delighted.[17]

This greatest of sustained metaphors is great because, secretly, Bunyan knows the power of the real thing. He can produce a metaphorical masterpiece because he has served an arduous apprenticeship on seventeenth-century cart tracks. And because he knows, any paragraph of his is worth an hour of insipid pilgrimage-parallels delivered by a pastor who has driven to church via the garden center and takes his vacation at Disneyland.

I've now spent a long time reading wild theological rants and cold theological treatises against pilgrimage. And they don't ring true. The rants are too hot; the treatises are too cold. They all try too hard. Some of them fear and distrust *experience* itself and where it might lead. Pilgrimage, particularly for some of the more uptight Protestants, is to be discouraged simply because you *feel* things when on pilgrimage, and feelings are unruly and hard to pen within narrow doctrinal tramlines. But something else is going on.

It is the ancient conflict of the sower and the herdsman, the settler and the nomad, Cain and Abel. The settlers came out on top, but they did so by killing the nomads. The guilt haunts them. The mark of Cain, intended for protection, is felt as a stigma. And indeed it is. It shouts to the world, but most deafeningly to the sons of Cain themselves, that sedentary Cain, feeling his true inferiority to his wandering brother and the sting of Yahweh's preference for the shepherd, became a murderer. Murderers are fearful people. They often kill people who know about their crimes and might expose them or, simply by existing, remind them of their intolerable guilt. Settlers know that their inheritance was won ignobly by bludgeoning their brothers to death. And they will kill anyone who reminds them of the fact, especially if the ones doing the reminding are the brothers' descendants.

The persecution of nomads and wanderers has been relentless. Sometimes it has been overt and brutal. The Nazis (arch-settlers, of course—their rhetoric was all about the "thousand-year Reich," and their obscene, grandiose buildings were the antithesis of a goatskin tent) rounded up those proverbially wandering Jews and gypsies and gassed them. As they looked those dying nomads in the eyes, the settlers knew that God had not changed his preference, and that enraged them all the more. Colonial powers of all kinds in Africa,

America, Australia, central Asia, and just about everywhere else, knowing that nomads, simply by existing, challenged the structures they were seeking to impose, hunted them down like dogs, claiming that they were not proper humans. The truth, of course, was that the nomads were particularly magnificent humans, whose humanity put the gun-wielding colonials to shame—a shame which at some level they felt.

Sometimes the persecution has been bureaucratic: try getting health care without a fixed address. Sometimes the settlers have used bribery: "Come and be one of us, and there will be wonderful things for you." The classic examples are the concentration of Bedouins in the Israeli Negev into settlements, native Americans into reservations, and Australian aborigines into their own towns. It never works. Central heating and a post office don't make up for the lost stars. So the nomads go walkabout, or if they stay in their cages, hit the bottle, giving the settlers another opportunity to say, "These are unrealized *untermenschen*: they are inferior to us." If deaths from alcohol and suicide are vertiginously higher among the Inuit than among the whites in neighboring settlements, does anybody really care? The answer is no, and the reason is the story of Cain and Abel.

Pilgrimage is a little pocket of nomadism. Many insecure societies, notably the "advanced" ones that have lost their connections with the land, and therefore fear it and its people, feel threatened. They worry that a little focus on pilgrimage might metastasize dangerously into settled life. They are right to worry.

The denouncers of pilgrimage are all (at least by the standards of their times) advanced urban intellectuals who have the most to lose. They are Cains, terrified of being reminded of what they have done, scared of the superior gaze of that favored, carefree, whistling boy as he walks past with his goats, mocking ever so slightly the serious, planning, budgeting older brother.

14

THE INEVITABLE PILGRIM

All of us are pilgrims on this earth; I have even heard
it said that the earth itself is a pilgrim in the heavens.

—Maxim Gorky[1]

God knows well who are the best pilgrims.

—Old English Proverb

"I've read some of your book," said Sarah, "and I find
it deeply offensive. All that stuff about how wanderers are superior to people who stay at home and more favored by God, and
how redemptive it is to walk. How do you think that makes me
feel?"

Sarah is forty-nine. In her early thirties she was diagnosed
with multiple sclerosis. She is now confined to a wheelchair.
The prognosis is not good. The journeys I have described are
impossible for her. She is tortured by the impossibility.

"You spend ages pouring scorn on 'metaphorical pilgrimages,'" she said, as close to being bitter as she could ever be.

"But that's all I can ever do. And if that makes me a second-class citizen of the kingdom you're always going on about, then I don't think I want to be a citizen at all. It doesn't sound like the sort of place I'd want to be."

Sarah is brilliant, learned, and wonderful, but she reads me wrong. She is a far more adventurous traveler than I have ever been or will ever be. When she goes to the shops in her electric wheelchair, she does a pilgrimage that is worth a hundred walks from Paris to Santiago. She's the nomad. Partly that is because she has a nomad's awareness of the transience of her present position. A nomad knows that he won't be geographically here tomorrow; his world is constantly changing, and so he sees it with those child's eyes. Sarah knows that she might not be biologically here next week, and the effect is the same. Her disease creates a terrifying newness each day.

I don't much like traveling these days. I hate to miss the sacred morning journey—the walk to school with Tom. I learn a lot on that journey. But when I start being impressed by the big names I know, or start to think that it is important to win or that the rich are really rich, then is the time to get up and walk and relearn the weird priorities of the kingdom.

If I have overstated the importance of walking along roads, I'm unrepentant, although sorry to have hurt Sarah and others like her. The physical business is important. It can never be otherwise for the mind-body-spirit cocktails we call humans. Ask Sarah. She is stretched physically to the limit by those trips to

the shops. Sarah doesn't need to walk to Rome. That's for many
reasons. Her MS has stripped her of the delusions that, for many
of us, need to be ground off on the tarmac. She would never,
ever, become dangerously attached to her work or her routine or
her home decorating plans. She knows the value of things. She
started to laugh at the suffocating careerism of the settlers in her
anarchic teens, and on the day of her diagnosis, the laugh became
deafening. She doesn't need help in learning the value of living
on the edge. That's where she's been for years. That the last will
be first, and the meek will inherit the earth are her only hopes.
They are everybody's only hopes, in fact, but she knows it.

"The book is all very well," said Victoria.

The Cain and Abel business is interesting, and I agree that
there's a disturbing bias to the margins in the teaching of
Jesus. But let's be realistic. We can't uproot the children from
school, buy a caravan and spend our life drifting between
trailer parks. I'm not sure what it would achieve, anyway. I
do a fair amount in the local church, and I don't think it's all
wasted. And as for solidarity with the downtrodden, what
would they like best? The check that our big fat jobs let us
send to charities every month, or a request to budge up and
make room for us all in some cardboard city or commune?

I'm not going to answer Victoria here, except to say that she can
and should take to the road for a week or two. There, on the edge

of the world for a while and without endangering her cash flow or her children's school places, she can taste the salt spray of the wild waves of the radical kingdom. Then, when she's back, we should talk. That spray is as addictive as crack cocaine.

The sort of pilgrimage I have been talking about in most of this book is most valuable for people who are not yet pilgrims, or have not yet realized that they are. Pilgrimages turn actual settlers into nomads and force closet nomads to come out. But once you are a wanderer, and know that you are, and feel Yahweh's pleasure and preference, you'll never, ever go back to being a settler, even if you never move from your office or living room again. The authorities can rip up your ID card, offer you the most extravagant incentives to go into a settlement, smash up your caravan, unscrew the Zyklon B, or offer you a seat on the board; and you'll give them the shepherd's smile and thumb your nose. Very graciously, of course, but with a humble knowledge of superiority.

You might find yourself drawn to do again the big journeys where you first learned to dance with the wandering God of the edges. Or you might find satisfying echoes of those journeys in day trips to local shrines, or processing around the stations of the cross in your local church. When I was last in Jerusalem, I went up to pray at the Western Wall. The cracks between the ancient stones are crammed full of notes with scribbled prayers. Some of the notes are very high up the wall. I am tall at six foot three, but on tiptoe and with outstretched arm, I was still more than a foot away from them. A very tall man standing on a chair must have put them there. Climbing onto that chair was a sacred journey.

"Can't you just say that we're all pilgrims?" urged Sarah. Well, yes, up to a point, we are. We are all proceeding inexorably through time, which appears to travel in more or less a straight line, to our deaths. However hard we try to insulate ourselves from change, however much Botox we pump into our faces, however much broccoli we eat, however often we have our prostates palpated, however prudent we are with our investments, however expensively we are insured, we will encounter changes analogous to those the pilgrim sees on the road. Whether those changes give us those new, childlike eyes and usher us into that crazy kingdom with its wild values, or instead shrink us harder into the hell that is ourselves, will depend on many things.

So yes, we're all pilgrims, but the metaphorical pilgrimage we're on might or might not do for us what an actual one probably will. It is too easy to read all the quotes that talk, in pretty much identical terms, about all life being a pilgrimage, and think, smugly and dangerously, that it means there's no urgency about getting up off the sofa and out onto the road.

"I just love this, from Van Gogh," said Hugh, a merchant banker in his thirties, taking a notebook out of his briefcase. "We are pilgrims on the earth, and strangers; we have come from afar and we are going far . . . The journey of our life goes from the loving breast of our Mother on earth to the arms of our Father in heaven. Everything on earth changes; we have no abiding

city here; it is the experience of everybody." He looked beatifi-
cally around, put the notebook down, took a swig of Chateau
Margaux, and moved on to tell us about the holiday home he'd
just bought in Tuscany.

This sort of thing is everywhere. Shakespeare's Henry IV
comforts himself with the thought that Jerusalem is wherever you
happen to decide it is. "It has been prophesied to me many years,
I should not die but in Jerusalem; which vainly I suppos'd the
Holy Land: But bear me to that chamber; there I'll lie; in that
Jerusalem shall Harry die."[2] "To set out boldly in our work is to
make a pilgrimage of our labors, to understand that the consummation of work lies not only in what we have done, but in
who we have become while accomplishing the task," notes David
Whyte.[3] "This world is but a thrughfare ful of woe, and we been
pilgrymes, passynge to and fro," Chaucer's Knight tells us.[4]

It's in the Bible too. In the passage where the Bible comes
nearest to gnosticism, we are told:

> Therefore from one person [Abraham] . . . descendants were
> born, "as many as the stars of heaven and as the innumer-
> able grains of sand by the seashore." All of these died in faith
> without having received the promises, but from a distance
> they saw and greeted them. They confessed that they were
> strangers and foreigners on the earth, for people who speak
> in this way make it clear that they are seeking a homeland. If
> they had been thinking of the land that they had left behind,

they would have had opportunity to return. But as it is, they desire a better country, that is, a heavenly one.[5]

"Strangers and foreigners on the earth"? "Seeking a homeland"? "Desire a better country, that is, a heavenly one"? This is no gnosticism, for the heavenly country spoken of is the supra-physical country populated by supra-sensual resurrection bodies, not by shades on clouds. But the writer is commending the nomadic state of mind as the only one that will keep you on the straight and narrow road. It's not a license for asceticism: "Strangers and foreigners" are the ones with the new eyes who see the colors of the world, the wonder and the power, who know the intimacy of real relationship, who walk and dance with the great stranger-foreigner-king.

Human beings are storytellers and storylisteners. I want to believe that I have a personal story, that I'm not an incoherent collection of episodes. God is apparently fond of stories, too, and particularly of traveling tales. If the Christians are right, I have a story, because God has made a traveling tale in which I am a character.

At the end of the road there will be a sense of homecoming, although the journey has been from A to B. "We shall not cease from exploration," wrote T. S. Eliot, "and the end of all our exploring will be to arrive where we started and know the place for the first time."[6] That's not completely true, if the Christians are right. It's too Eastern. The nomadic people of God, if they're on the right road, go from an oasis somewhere in East Africa, Mesopotamia, or the Jungian collective subconscious (depending on your exegetical preferences) through wild and barren places, progressively learning to smile, relate, and serve. And they end up in a city where none of their desert sensibilities are violated, where everything they have learned about self-giving and relationship is used and multiplied and transformed.

Everything moves. We move too. Either willingly or unwillingly. Go willingly, and the business is redemptive and joyful. Go unwillingly, and the stream will dash and drown you.

The Buddha's last words to his disciples were "Walk on." The first words of Jesus to his were rather different: "Follow me." Jesus said some other things, too, but as a summary of the four Gospels, "Let's go for a walk together" is not bad.

If who happens to read this work judges it to be useful, that will be my reward for the work I have done, and I shall regard it as a precious prize. But if otherwise, let my offspring return to me, its begetter. With its stammers may it remind me of these Holy Places, so that I can recreate their memory in my mind. For that, too, will be a sweet delight.

—JOHN PHOCAS, TWELFTH-CENTURY PILGRIM TO JERUSALEM

STUDY GUIDE
The Sacred Journey
Charles Foster

"Stand at the crossroads and look; ask for the ancient paths, ask where the good way is, and walk in it, and you will find rest for your souls."

JEREMIAH 6:16

Prologue, Chapter 1: The Strange Strider

In your answer to the question at the end of the prologue, what part of your own faith experience played a part in your choices?

Most believers who make a pilgrimage to the Holy Land return significantly changed. Have you or anyone you know visited Jerusalem? How did experiences there change how they (or you) see the relationship with God?

Chapter 2: The Kingdom Road: A Theology for Walkers

Why do you think that the actual journey of a pilgrimage can be as life-changing as the destination?

Do you have difficulty thinking of Jesus as fully human, as the author describes, with sore feet and hunger pangs? In what way do you think Jesus' humanity influences our desire to travel?

Chapter 3: Bias to the Wanderer

As the author goes through the story of the Old Testament from the point of view of the wanderer, how do you respond to his idea that it is spiritually healthier to wander than to settle in towns and cities? In what ways can we keep the spirit of the nomad even as we maintain a home and honor responsibilities?

In what ways is our nomadic nature revealed in the advice we give during a crisis, such as "take one step at a time"? How does this show our beliefs in the healing nature of the journey?

Chapter 4: The God Who Walks

With Jesus' own ministry covered over in traveling verbs, He sets a high standard when it comes to taking the message to the people. How do we follow in His steps when we have to be at soccer practice every Monday, Wednesday, and Friday?

Chapter 5: Why Go? Getting Rid of Junk

If you could make your most desired pilgrimage, what elements in your life would you want to see sloughed away— sins, anchoring possessions, broken relationships?

Chapter 6: Why Go? Thirst for an Encounter

While most of us would not undertake a pilgrimage in search of relics, many do start with distinct notions about God. How would your world, your beliefs change if the God you find on your pilgrimage differs vastly from the God you expected to encounter?

Does this happen to us even at home, when we discover God working in some new and unexpected way in our world?

Chapter 7: Where To? Thin Places

Are there "thin places" in your life, where you have felt closer to God? What makes those places special to you? Why do you think you are more open to God's presence in those locations?

Chapter 8: Packing and Preparation

How light would you be willing to travel? Can you freely go without your computer, make-up or hair dryer, books or mp3 player? What other non-essentials of life tie you down?

Chapter 9: The Journey: Old Feet, New Eyes

When you travel a road or walk a path for the first time, it can seem longer and more vibrant than when you've traversed it the second, fifth, or fiftieth time. The first time you see it as a child, with fresh eyes. Likewise, a pilgrimage can help us refresh that first love we had for Christ and overcome a fear of the unknown.

How can we bring this freshness home, keeping what we've learned once we've returned to our everyday world? Are there routines in your life now that lock you into a fear of change, of a refreshed relationship with God?

Chapter 10: The Journey: Blistered Feet, Tired Eyes

For those of us who have become dependent on daily comforts, conditions on a pilgrimage can come as a shock. In what ways can we stay open and vulnerable to what God has to show us without abandoning common sense about our personal safety?

Would you be open to the adventure of an unplanned trip, without time tables and daily goals?

Chapter 11: The Fellowship of the Road

Have you ever taken a trip (or a pilgrimage) that put you in close contact with people completely different? In what way does being with strangers make you vulnerable, more open to the lessons of God? In what way could you seek this out closer to home, without striking out on foot for Santiago?

Chapter 12: Arrival and Return

A pilgrimage is more than the journey to and arrival at your destination. It is also about the return. As the author points out, pilgrimage changes people—and it should. How do you translate the growth, the experiences, the new awareness of the journey into an ongoing relationship with God and those around you?

How do you transform the pilgrimage to a place into your life's journey?

Chapter 13: "It's a Profane Journey": Opponents of Pilgrimage

"Why bother?" How would you answer the critics of your proposed pilgrimage, whether to the Holy Land or a sacred place closer to home?

Chapter 14: The Inevitable Pilgrim

A pilgrimage isn't about distance; it's about traveling to the edge, about leaving behind and allowing time or geography or hardships or illness slough off those things that bind us mind and spirit to the non-essential parts of our lives—that which keeps us from fully stepping alongside Jesus when He looks into our eyes and says, "Come, let's take a walk."

So . . . what physical pilgrimage do you need to make? What will make you see the world with fresh eyes, tired feet, and a mind open to whatever new experiences God has in store?

NOTES

Chapter 1

1. Luke 9:58.
2. Genesis 12:1, 4.
3. Exodus 34:23.
4. Qur'an 3:98.
5. There are, of course, plenty of local Islamic shrines much used by pilgrims. But it can be contended forcefully that these shrines prove that purity of doctrine requires some sort of central rule. Folk Islam draws much of its strength from these smaller shrines.
6. Constantine became emperor in AD 306. The Edict of Milan, AD 313, proclaimed religious toleration throughout the Empire.
7. Matthew 27:51.
8. Ezekiel 47:1.
9. Christian pilgrimage to the Holy Land is generally thought to have begun in the second century. The first detailed account we have from a Christian pilgrim there is that of the *Bordeaux Pilgrim*, written in 333.
10. The meaning of *Domine ivimus* is contentious. *Ivimus* is an archaic—or at least poetic—form of the first person plural active indicative of *ire*. This is a form usually adopted by Golden- and Silver-age poets for metrical purposes, but it's also quite characteristic of rhetorical or lapidary Latin: the added *v* lends it a sonorous quality. But the labial consonants *b* and *v* became philologically interchangeable at some point in the evolution of Vulgate Latin, and so *Domine ivimus* could mean either "Lord, we have arrived," or "Lord, we came," or alternatively, "Lord, we will come to you." In support of the latter reading, one might contend that there is an echo of Psalm 122:1: "I was glad when they said to me, 'Let us go to the house of the LORD!'"

Chapter 2

1. Martyn Layzell, "As Jesus Walked" (Thankyou Music: Nashville, 2005).
2. C. S. Lewis, *The Lion, the Witch and the Wardrobe* (London: Geoffrey Bles), 1950.
3. Kelly Carpenter, "You're All I Want" (Mercy/Vineyard Publishing: Nashville, 1994).
4. "Be Thou My Vision," trans. Mary E. Byrne (1905), versified Eleanor H. Hull (1912).
5. One journey Jesus talked about was a missionary journey: "Go therefore and make disciples of all nations." What is the gospel that we are meant to take with us on that journey? Matthew tells us that we are to baptize them and teach them "to obey everything that [Jesus has] commanded" (Matt. 28:19–20). And what did he command? We are back to Matthew 10 and Luke 10—the command to go out and

proclaim and demonstrate that the kingdom of heaven has come near (Matt.10:1–15). Similarly for the seventy (Luke 10:1–12; c. Luke 24:47).

6. Romans 1:16.
7. Romans 3:23.
8. Matthew 4:17.
9. You might try to make a case for it from the Zacchaeus story, "Today salvation has come to this house" (Luke 19:9); from the thief on the cross (Luke 23:43); or from the story of "doubting" Thomas, "My Lord and my God!" (John 20:28). The argument is of course stronger from Acts.
10. Acts 2:47.
11. The disciples got the point eventually, of course.
12. "You believe that God is one; you do well. Even the demons believe—and shudder" (James 2:19).
13. And matters very much. For instance: Matthew 7:24; Luke 9:26; John 3:36; 6:63.
14. Matthew 25:35–42.
15. Matthew 6:26.
16. Paulo Coelho, *O didrio de um Mago*. Rio de Janeiro: Editora Rocco, 1987. Translated by Paulo Coelho and Alan R. Clarke as *The Pilgrimage* (San Francisco: HarperCollins, 1995), 248.
17. John G. Neihardt, *Black Elk Speaks: Being the Life Story of a Holy Man of the Oglala Sioux* (Lincoln: University of Nebraska Press, 1988), 150.
18. Phyllis Tickle, *The Great Emergence: How Christianity Is Changing and Why* (Grand Rapids, MI: Baker Books, 2008), chap. 1.
19. It only appears three times. See Acts 11:26; 26:28; 1 Peter 4:16.

Chapter 3

1. Charles Darwin. *Origin of certain instincts. Nature. A Weekly Illustrated Journal of Science* 7 (3 April 1873), 417–418.
2. Democritus Junior [Robert Burton], *The Anatomy of Melancholy*, (London: Duckworth and Co., 1905) 2:167.
3. Genesis 1:1–2:3; cf. Genesis 2:4–25.
4. Genesis 1:31.
5. Genesis 2:15.
6. Genesis 4:1–22.
7. Not in Genesis, anyway. Hebrews 11:4 says, "By faith Abel offered to God a more acceptable sacrifice than Cain's. Through this he received approval as righteous, God himself giving approval to his gifts; he died, but through his faith he still speaks."
8. Genesis 4:14, 15. I have commented in *The Selfless Gene* (Nashville: Thomas Nelson, 2010), on the fact that if the Genesis account is to be taken literally, the only other people on the earth were his father and mother, who were unlikely to try to kill him.
9. C. S. Lewis, *The Magician's Nephew*, (London: Bodley Head, 1955).
10. Leon Kass, *The Beginning of Wisdom* (Chicago: University of Chicago Press, 2003). Several of the ideas in this chapter are inspired by it.

11. See, for instance, Ezekiel 29:9: "The land of Egypt shall be a desolation and a waste. Then they shall know that I am the LORD. Because you said, 'The Nile is mine, and I made it.'"
12. Luke 12:13–23.
13. Genesis 11:8.
14. Genesis 12:1–4.
15. Søren Kierkegaard to Jette, 1847, cited in Bruce Chatwin, *The Songlines* (London: Franklin,1986).
16. Exodus 12:8.
17. Exodus 20:24, 25.
18. Deuteronomy 34:6.
19. Deuteronomy 26:1, 5.
20. Jeremiah 35:7.
21. Jeremiah 35:1–19.
22. Chatwin, *The Songlines*, 195.
23. Laurens Van der Post, *The Lost World of the Kalahari* (New York: Morrow, 1958).
24. Genesis 18:1–8.
25. Genesis 19:1–29.
26. Genesis 19:7–8.
27. *Aitareya Brahmana* 7:15.
28. Henry David Thoreau, *Walden; Or, Life in the Woods* (Boston: Ticknor and Fields, 1854).
29. Robert Louis Stevenson, *Travels with a Donkey in the Cevennes* (London: Electric Book, 2001), 46.
30. Luke 1:53.

Chapter 4

1. Friedrich Nietzsche, *Thus Spoke Zarathustra: A Book for All and None*, trans. Thomas Common (n.p.: Forgotten Books, 2008), 37.
2. Matthew 1:17. There is a mysterious miscounting in relation to the final set of fourteen generations. But the writer of Matthew was no fool. I explore the anomaly in *The Christmas Mystery* (Colorado Springs, CO: Authentic Books, 2007).
3. Matthew 2:1–2.
4. Matthew 2:9.
5. Matthew 2:1–12.
6. Matthew 2:13.
7. I suspect that they avoided the main route through the wilderness, which met the Via Maris at Ashkelon, and instead used obscure tracks whenever they could.
8. Matthew 2:23.
9. John 1:46.
10. Matthew 3:7–9.
11. Matthew 3:4–5.
12. Matthew 3:3, emphasis added.

13. Matthew 3:5.
14. Matthew 3:13.
15. Matthew 4:1.
16. Matthew 4:12.
17. Matthew 4:18.
18. Matthew 4:22, emphasis added.
19. Matthew 4:23.
20. Matthew 4:24–25.
21. Matthew 6:10–11, emphasis added.
22. Matthew 6:25–26.
23. Matthew 6:34.
24. Matthew 7:8.
25. Matthew 7:13–14.
26. Matthew 9:9.
27. Matthew 9:27.
28. Matthew 9:35.
29. Matthew 10:5–15. These instructions are echoed for the seventy in Luke 10:1–16.
30. Matthew 11:3.
31. Matthew 11:4–5.
32. Matthew 12:9.
33. Matthew 12:15.
34. Matthew 15:21.
35. Matthew 15:29.
36. Matthew 16:13.
37. Matthew 19:1.
38. Matthew 20:17.
39. Matthew 20:29.
40. Matthew 21:1.
41. Matthew 21:10.
42. Matthew 10:38–39.
43. Matthew 2:13, 23; 4:25; 6:4; 12:1, 20; 13:1, 29; 18:28–29; 19:14.
44. John 7:1–14, 37. John also notes Jesus' observance of Chanukah (10:22) and an unnamed festival (5:1).
45. Luke 1:39–40.
46. Chatwin, *The Songlines*, 229 .
47. Luke 2:1–7.
48. Luke 2:8–18.
49. The historicity of the traditional nativity site is discussed in detail in *The Christmas Mystery* (Colorado Springs, CO: Authentic Books, 2007).
50. Luke 2:16.
51. Luke 2:15.
52. Luke 2:20.
53. Luke 2:41–42.
54. Luke 17:20–21.
55. Luke 24:15–32.
56. Revelation 21:9–25.

57. It is almost enough to propel a man into Platonism after all. But not quite. Be careful.
58. Revelation 22:17.

Chapter 5

1. "The Voyage of the Ui Chorra," *Immrama*.
2. A plenary indulgence gives remission from all suffering in Purgatory. William Wey, *The Itineraries of William Wey, Fellow at Eton College: The Jerusalem, AD 1458 and AD 1462* (London: J. B. Nichols and Son, 1857).
3. C. H. Spurgeon, "Scala Santa," *Sword and Trowel* (London: Passmore and Alabaster, 1874).
4. C. S. Lewis, *A Grief Observed* (London: Faber and Faber, 1961), 66.
5. Quoted in Ian Bradley, *Pilgrimage* (Oxford: Lion Publishing, 2009), 201.
6. *Aitareya Brahmana* 7:15.
7. Proverbs 5:8.
8. Genesis 39:12.
9. Luke 14:26. See also Matthew 19:29; Mark 10:29.
10. Matthew 16:25.
11. Caroline Friend, *A Time of Miracles, in Pilgrimage*, ed. Ruth Barnes and Crispin Branfoot (Oxford: Ashmolean Museum, 2006), 118–129.
12. Mark Twain, *The Innocents Abroad* (New York: Harper, 1906), 444.
13. John Bunyan, *The Pilgrim's Progress*, rev. ed. (1678, 1684, repr., New York: Scott, Foresman and Co., 1922), 47.
14. Mahabharata 3.33.80.
15. "Hymn of Guru Arjan Dev," in *Title of Compilation*, trans. name (City: Publisher, date).
16. H. R. R. Gill and C. F. Beckingham trans., *The Travels of Ibn Battuta* (London: Hakluyt Society, 1958–2000).
17. "The Hermit," in *A Celtic Miscellany: Translations from the Celtic Literatures*, trans. Kenneth Hurlstone Jackson (Harmondsworth, UK: Penguin, 1971), 281–282.
18. C. S. Lewis, *Voyage of the Dawn Treader*, Collectors Ed. (New York: HarperCollins, 2006) 244.
19. Jeremiah 29:13, author's translation.
20. C. S. Lewis, *Letters to Malcolm, Chiefly on Prayer: Reflections on the Intimate Dialogue Between Man and God* (London: Harcourt, Brace and World, 1964), 106–7.
21. Psalm 24:3–4.

Chapter 6

1. Celedabhaill, *Annals of the Masters*, part 3, M926.5.
2. Valerius, a seventh-century Galician monk, urging his fellow monks to emulate the great pilgrim nun, Egeria, in *Memorable Deeds and Sayings*, trans. H. J. Walker (Indianapolis: Hackett, 2004).
3. Geoffrey Chaucer, "Prologue," *Canterbury Tales*, fragment1, lines 1–18.

4. *Martyrdom of Polycarp*, 18.2.
5. Andrew Boorde, *Fyrst Boke of the Introduction of Knowledge*, Early English Text Society (London: N. Trubner and Co., 1870), 204.
6. Erasmus, *Colloquy*, trans. John rough Nichols (London: Nichols and Sons, 1875), 39–52.
7. 2 Kings 13:20–21.
8. Acts 19:11–12.
9. Gill and Beckingham, *The Travels of Ibn Battuta*.
10. Robert M. Pirsig, *Zen and the Art of Motorcycle Maintenance* (New York: William Morrow, 1974), 13.
11. For detailed discussion of "Jerusalem Syndrome," see Charles Foster, *Wired for God: The Biology of Spiritual Experience* (London: Hodder, 2010).

Chapter 7

1. T. S. Eliot. *Four Quartets* (New York 1943; Great Britain 1944; repr., New York: Harvest Books, 1968), 39.
2. "Tudur Aled," in T. Charles-Edwards, *Saint Winefride and Her Well: The Historical Background* (London: CTS, 1968).
3. John of Wurzburg, *Descriptio terra sanctae*, in ed. John Wilkinson, *Jerusalem Pilgrimage 1099-1185* (London: Hakluyt Society, 1988).
4. Andrew Harvey, *Hidden Journey: A Spiritual Awakening* (London: Bloomsbury, 1991).
5. For a detailed discussion of the origins and significance of the cave art of the Upper Palaeolithic, see Charles Foster, *Wired for God: The Biology of Spiritual Experience* (London: Hodder, 2010).
6. Vyasa Maharshi. "Kashi Khanda," *Skanda Purana*.
7. Jose Ortega y Gasset, *La pedagogia del paisaje*.
8. Midrash Tanehuma, Leviticus 10.
9. Jacques de Vitry, *Historia orientalis* (repr., Melsenheim am Glan, 1971), 215.
10. Wey, *The Itineraries of William Wey*.
11. Zohar, Exodus 15:17.
12. Matthew 6:21; Luke 12:34.

Chapter 8

1. Henry David Thoreau, *Walden; or Life in the Woods* (Boston: Houghton, Mifflin, and Co., 1893), 144.
2. Wey, *The Itineraries of William Wey*.
3. Lao Tzu, *Tao Te Ching*, 64, line 2.
4. This quotation was mistakenly attributed to Johann Goethe by William Hutchinson Murray in his travel log *The Scottish Himalyan Expedition* (London: J. M. Dent and Sons, 1951).
5. See also Mark 6:9; Luke 9:3.
6. Wey, *Itineraries*.
7. Boorde, *Fyrst Boke of the Introduction of Knowledge*, 219.

8. Saint Brendan of Clonfert, *The Voyage of St. Brendan*, in Rev. Denis O'Donoghue, *Brendaniana: St. Brendan the Voyager in Story and Legend* (Dublin: Brown and Nolin, 1893), 104–78.

9. Amir Soltai Sheikholeslami, quoted in Edward Sellner, *Pilgrimage: Exploring a Great Spiritual Practice* (Notre Dame, IN: Soren Books, 2004), 114.

10. Thomas Merton, *Mystics and Zen Masters* (New York: Farrar, Straus, and Giroux, 1967; repr., 1999), 226.

Chapter 9

1. Paulo Coelho, *The Pilgrimage* (San Francisco: HarperOne, 1995), 121.
2. Freya Stark *Alexander's Path* (Orlando: Harcourt, Brace and World, 1958).
3. Albert Camus, *The Rebel: An Essay on Man in Revolt* (London: Vintage, 1992), 11.
4. Ibid.
5. Coelho, *The Pilgrimage*, 118.
6. Augustine, *Confessions*, 10.35.
7. Thomas à Kempis, *The Imitation of Christ*, trans. Leo Sherley-Price (London: Penguin, 1952), 186.

Chapter 10

1. Alex Garland, *The Beach* (London: Penguin, 1996).
2. *Saewulf*, trans. W. R. Brownlow (London: Palestine Pilgrims' Text Society, 1896).
3. John Bunyan, *The Pilgrim's Progress*, rev. ed. (1678, 1684; repr., London: Penguin, 2009) 116–17.
4. Quoted in John Ure, *Pilgrimage: The Great Adventure of the Middle Ages* (London: Constable, 2006), 9.
5. Bunyan, *Pilgrim's Progress*, 115.
6. Ibid., 91–92.
7. John Bunyan, *The Pilgrim's Progress*, rev. ed. (1678, 1684; repr., New York: Scott, Foresman and Co., 1922).
8. Quoted in John Ure, *Pilgrimage*, 57.
9. Hans von Mergenthal, quoted in Pietro Casola, *Pilgrimage to Jerusalem in the Year 1494*, trans. M. Margaret Newett (Manchester: Manchester Univ. Press, 1907), 91.
10. Casola, *Pilgrimage to Jerusalem in the Year 1494*, 194.
11. von Mergenthal, Pilgrimage, 91.
12. Casola, *Pilgrimage*, 157.
13. Ibid., 161.
14. Arculf, *The Pilgrimage of Arcultus in the Holy Land*, trans. J. M. McPherson (London: Palestine Pilgrims' Text Society, 1889), 3–4.
15. "We also rejoice in our sufferings, because we know that suffering produces perseverance" (Romans 5:3 NIV). The NRSV says, "We also boast in our sufferings."

16. Quoted in John Ure, *Pilgrimage*, 9.
17. Saint Brendan of Clonfert, *The Voyage of St. Brendan*, in Rev. Denis O'Donoghue, *Brendaniana: St. Brendan the Voyager in Story and Legend* (Dublin: Brown and Nolin, 1893), 104–78.
18. Dag Hammarskjold, *Markings*, trans. Leif Sjoberg and W. H. Auden (trans) (London Faber and Faber: 1964).
19. Hebrews 9:27, author's interpretation.
20. Mother Teresa (Agnes Gonxha Bojaxhiu), http://www.time.com/time/world/article/0,8599,1655415,00.html.
21. Ibid.
22. Saint Brendan of Clongert, *Voyage*, 104–78.
23. Matthew 7:7; Luke 11:9.
24. Romans 8:28.
25. See note, p. 165.
26. Saint Brendan of Clongert, *Voyage*, 104–78.
27. Joseph Campbell, quoted in Cousineau, *The Art of Pilgrimage*, 75.
28. Meister Eckhart, quoted in Phil Cousineau, *The Art of Pilgrimage*, 80.

Chapter 11
1. Paulo Coelho, *The Pilgrimage* (London: HarperCollins, 1997).
2. Quoted in Joe Darion, "The Impossible Dream," *Man of La Mancha* (1972).
3. Deuteronomy 26:5.
4. John Bunyan, *The Pilgrim's Progress*, rev. ed. (1678, 1684, repr., New York: Scott, Foresman and Co., 1922).
5. Mark 1:15.
6. William of Malmesbury records how the bones of St. John of Beverley inhibited the a natural savagery of bulls and bulldogs. They would not fight in the churchyard of Beverley Minster.
7. Matthew 6:26, author's interpretation.
8. A good case can be made for her suffering from migraine, as it is widely supposed did Hildegard of Bingen. Margery describes hearing "with her bodily ears such sounds and melodies that she could not hear what anyone said to her at that time unless she spoke louder," and "she saw with her bodily eyes many white things flying all about her . . . as specks in a sunbeam . . . and the brighter the sun shone, the better she could see them." Quoted in Sarah Hopper, *Mothers, Mystics and Merrymakers* (Gloucestershire, UK: Sutton, 2006), 47.
9. Casola, *Pilgrimage to Jerusalem in the Year 1494*.
10. Felix Fabri, *The Wanderings of Felix Fabri*, A. Stewart trans., (London: Palestine Pilgrims' Text Society,1983).

Chapter 12
1. Bunyan, *The Pilgrim's Progress*, rev. ed. (1678, 1684, repr., New York: Scott, Foresman and Co., 1922).

2. R. S. Thomas, "Migrants," in *Mass for Hard Times* (Tarset: Bloodaxe, 1993).
3. Psalm 137:4.
4. Luke 19:40, author translation.
5. Jerome to Eustochium, 108.
6. John Wilkinson, Joyce Hill, W. F. Ryan, eds., *Jerusalem Pilgrimage, 1099–1185,* (London: Hakluyt Society, 1999).
7. Fabri, *The Wanderings of Felix Fabri.*
8. Herman Melville, *Journal of a Visit to Europe and the Levant* (1857, repr., Princeton, NJ: Princeton Univ. Press, 1955), 281.
9. W. H. Bartlett, *Jerusalem Revisited* (London: T. Nelson and Sons, 1876).
10. Caroline Friend, "A Time of Miracles," *Pilgrimage,* eds. Ruth Barnes and Crispin Branfoot (Oxford: Ashmolean Museum, 2006).
11. Shirley du Boulay, *The Road to Canterbury: A Modern Pilgrimage* (New York: Morehouse, 1995).
12. Thomas Merton, *The Asian Journal* (New York: New Directions, 1975), 235–36.
13. R. S. Thomas, *Collected Poems 1945-1990* (London: Dent, 1993), 91.
14. Phil Cousineau, *The Art of Pilgrimage* (Berkeley, CA: Conari, 1998), 222. Emphasis original.
15. Luke 15:11–32.
16. Matthew 13:57. See also Mark 6:4: "Prophets are not without honor, except in their hometown, and among their own kin, and in their own house." Luke 4:24: "Truly I tell you, no prophet is accepted in the prophet's hometown."

Chapter 13

1. Dennis Silk, *Retrievements: A Jerusalem Anthology* (Jerusalem: Keter Publishing House, 1977).
2. Celia Fiennes, *Of Pilgrims to Holywell* (North Wales, 1698).
3. Quoted in Charlotte Vaudeville, *A Weaver Called Kabir* (Delhi: Oxford Univ. Press, 1997), 217–18.
4. Martin Luther, *To the Christian Nobility of the German Nations, Concerning the Improvement of the Condition of the Christian Culture,* trans. Charles M. Jacobs, R Luther (Minneapolis: Fortress Press, 1970).
5. John Wycliffe, quoted in John Laird Wilson, *John Wycliffe, Patriot and Reformer: The Morning Star of the Reformation* (New York: Funk and Wagnalls, 1884), 105.
6. William Umpton, quoted in *Letters and Papers, Foreign and Domestic, of the Reign of Henry VIII, 1509-47,* vol. 5, no. 1271 (London: 1862–1910), 202.
7. There were often concerns about the moral dangers of pilgrimage. The Synod of Friuli (c. 795) forbade nuns from going on pilgrimage: "And at no time whatsoever shall it be permitted to any abbess or nun to go to Rome or to tour other holy places, if Satan should transform himself into an angel of light and suggest it to them as if for the purpose of

prayer. No one is so obtuse or stupid as to be unaware how irreligious and reprehensible it is [for them] to have dealings with men on account of the necessities of travel." Quoted in Sarah Hopper, *Mothers, Mystics and Merrymakers* (Gloucestershire, UK: Sutton, 2006), 47.

8. William Thorpe, Examination of William Thorpe (OD col.), 140–141.

9. Quoted in *Reflecting at Knock . . . Before Our Personal Lamb*, by Tom Lane (New York: Columbia Univ. Press, 2007).

10. Jeremiah 29:13–14.

11. Abu Said, quoted in Peter J. Awn, "The Ethical Concerns of Classical Sufiism," *Journal of Religious Ethics*, 11:2 (Fall 1983), 240–63.

12. Kabir, quoted in Simon Coleman and John Elsner, *Pilgrimages: Past and Present in World Religions* (Italy, 1995), 153.

13. Jerome, Letter 58.

14. Gregory of Nyssa, quoted in Dore Gold, *The Fight for Jerusalem: Radical Islam, the West, and the Future of the Holy City* (Washington: Regnery, 2007), 67.

15. Abbess Samthann, quoted in David Adam, *The Road of Life: Reflections on Searching and Longing* (London: Society for Promoting Christian Knowledge, 2004), 113.

16. John Bunyan, *The Pilgrim's Progress*, rev. ed. (1678, 1684, repr., New York: Scott, Foresman and Co., 1922).

17. Ibid.

Chapter 14

1. Maxim Gorky, *The Lower Depths*, A. Bakshy and P. S. Nathan trans., (New Haven: Yale University Press, 1959).

2. William Shakespeare, *Henry IV*, part 2, 4.5.

3. David Whyte, *Crossing the Unknown Sea: Work as a Pilgrimage of Identity* (New York: Penguin, 2002), 5.

4. Geoffrey Chaucer, "The Knight," *Canterbury Tales*, fragment 1, lines 1989–90.

5. Hebrews 11:12–16.

6. T. S. Eliot. *Four Quartets* (New York 1943; Great Britain 1944), 47.

SELECT BIBLIOGRAPHY

The literature of pilgrimage is vast. This list contains just a few of the important books. Most of the books on the list are histories, anthropological and theological discussions, and anthologies, rather than accounts of specific pilgrimage sites. There is a sprinkling of personal and devotional accounts.

Adair, John. *The Pilgrims' Way*. London: Book Club Associates, 1978.

Barnes, Ruth and Branfoot, Crispin, eds. *Pilgrimage: The Sacred Journey*. Oxford: Ashmolean Museum, 2006.

Bartholomew, Craig and Hughes, Fred. *Explorations in a Christian Theology of Pilgrimage*. Aldershot: Ashgate, 2004.

Bradley, Ian. *Pilgrimage: A Spiritual and Cultural Journey*. Oxford: Lion, 2009.

Plate, Brent S., ed. *The Varieties of Contemporary Pilgrimage*. CrossCurrents, Vol. 59(3), 260-397, 2009.

Bunyan, John. *Pilgrim's Progress*. Numerous editions.

Butler, Barbara and White, Jo. *To Be a Pilgrim*. Stowmarket: Kevin Mayhew, 2002.

Calamari, Barbara, and DiPasqua, Sandra. *Holy Places: Sacred Sites in Catholicism*. New York: Viking Studio, 2002.

Chatwin, Bruce. *The Songlines*. London: Franklin, 1986.

Chaucer, Geoffrey. *The Canterbury Tales*. Numerous editions.

Coelho, Paulo. *The Pilgrimage*. London: HarperCollins, 1997.

Coleman, Simon, and Elsner, John. *Pilgrimage: Past and Present in the World Religions*. Cambridge: Harvard University Press, 1995.

Cousineau, Phil. *The Art of Pilgrimage*. Berkeley, California: Conari, 1998.

Davies, J. G. *Pilgrimage Yesterday and Today: Why? Where? How?* London: SCM Press, 1988.

Eade, John and Sallnow, Michael, eds. *Contesting the Sacred: The Anthropology of Christian Pilgrimage*. Routledge: Abingdon, 1991.

Fladmark, Magnus, ed. *In search of Heritage as Pilgrim or Tourist?* Shaftesbury: Donhead, 1998.

French, R. M. *The Way of a Pilgrim: And the Pilgrim Continues His Way*. San Franciso: HarperSanFranciso, 1991. (Translation of anonymous Russian original.)

Galland, China. *Longing for Darkness: Tara and the Black Madonna*. New York: Penguin, 1990.

Harpur, James. *Sacred Tracks: 2000 years of Christian Pilgrimage*. Berkeley, CA: University of California Press, 2002.

Henderson, P., ed. *A Pilgrim Anthology*. London: Confraternity of St. James, 1994.

Hopper, Sarah. *Mothers, Mystics and Merrymakers: Mediaeval Women Pilgrims*. Stroud: Sutton, 2006.

Lee, Mary and Nolan, Sidney. *Christian Pilgrimage in Modern Western Europe*. Chapel Hill: University of North Carolina Press, 1989.

Mahoney, Rosemary. *The Singular Pilgrim: Travels on Sacred Ground*. Boston: Houghton Mifflin, 2003.

Merton, Thomas. *The Seven Storey Mountain*. New York: Harcourt Brace Jovanovich, 1948.

Morris, Colin and Roberts, Peter, eds. *Pilgrimage: The English Experience from Becket to Bunyan*. Cambridge: Cambridge University Press, 2002.

Munro, Eleanor. *On Glory Roads: A Pilgrim's Book About Pilgrimage*. London: Thames and Hudson, 1987.

Pemberton, Cintra. *Soulfaring*. Harrisburg, PA: Morehouse.

Pentkovksy, Aleksei, ed. *The Pilgrim's Tale*. New York: Paulist Press, 1999.

Robinson, Martin. *Sacred Places, Pilgrim Paths: An Anthology of Pilgrimage*. New York: HarperCollins, 1995.

Sellner, Edward. *Pilgrimage*. Notre Dame, IN: Sorin Books, 2004.

Sheldrake, Philip. *Living Between Worlds*. London: Darton Longman and Todd, 1995.

Simpson, Ray. *A Pilgrim Way: New Celtic Monasticism for Everyday People*. Stowmarket: Kevin Mayhew, 2005.

Skevington, Andrea. *The Pilgrim Spirit*. Oxford: Lion Hudson, 2007.

Sumption, Jonathan. *Pilgrimage: An Image of Mediaeval Religion*. London: Faber, 1975.

Turner, Victor. *Image and Pilgrimage in Christian Culture: Anthropological Perspectives*. Oxford: Blackwell, 1978.

Ure, John, *Pilgrimage: The Great Adventure of the Middle Ages*. London: Constable, 2006.

Vest, Douglas. *On Pilgrimage*. Cambridge, MA: Cowley, 1998.

Webb, Diana. *Pilgrims and Pilgrimage in the Mediaeval West*. London: Longman, 2000.

Westwood, Jennifer. *On Pilgrimage: Sacred Journeys Around the world*. Mahwah, NJ: Hidden Spring, 2003.

Whyte, David. *Crossing the Unknown Sea: Work as a Pilgrimage of Identity*. New York: Riverhead, 2001.

Wilkinson, John, ed. *Jerusalem Pilgrimage 1099–1185*. London: Hakluyt Society, 1988.

ABOUT THE AUTHOR

Charles Foster is a writer, barrister, tutor in medical law and ethics at the University of Oxford, and a Fellow of Green Templeton College, Oxford. He has written, edited, or contributed to more than thirty books.

THE ANCIENT PRACTICES SERIES

PHYLLIS TICKLE, GENERAL EDITOR

Finding Our Way Again by Brian McLaren

In Constant Prayer by Robert Benson

Sabbath by Dan B. Allender

Fasting by Scot McKnight

Tithing by Douglas LeBlanc

The Sacred Meal by Nora Gallagher

The Liturgical Year by Joan Chittister

The Sacred Journey by Charles Foster

Stand at the crossroads and look; ask for the ancient paths,
ask where the good way is, and walk in it,
and you will find rest for your souls.

—JEREMIAH 6:16 NIV

THOMAS NELSON
Since 1798